FRANCE
THE NEW REPUBLIC
by Raymond Aron

Introduction by D. W. Brogan

Published for The Fund for the Republic, Inc.

by

Oceana Publications
New York

Library of Congress Catalog Card Number: 59-12292

PRINTED IN THE U.S.A.

TABLE OF CONTENTS

PREFACE

In their study of the nature and purposes of a free society and how it may be maintained in twentieth century America, the Consultants on the Basic Issues to the Fund for the Republic invited Raymond Aron to join them during their meetings in October of 1958 for a discussion of the new Constitution which had just been drafted for the Fifth Republic of France. The Consultants believed that Professor Aron's views on the new Constitution for his country would contribute to their own examination of the American Constitution and its applicability to the problems of our society. Their belief was justified.

Professor Aron's presentation is now offered in book form, together with some of the discussion that followed his talk, because the sponsors and the publisher think that the material will be of interest to a wider audience.

The Consultants on the Basic Issues to the Fund for the Republic are A. A. Berle, Jr., Scott Buchanan, Eugene Burdick, Eric F. Goldman, Clark Kerr, Henry R. Luce, John Courtney Murray, S.J., Reinhold Niebuhr, and Isidor I. Rabi.

ROBERT M. HUTCHINS

INTRODUCTION

Constitutions, like books, have their own history and destiny, and brief as has been the life of the new French Constitution it has already shown signs of developing in ways that cannot have been wholly foreseen by the drafters. The very fact that the Constitution was born of a crisis ensured that unexpected developments would take place, since the crisis did not come simply to an end with the adoption of the Constitution but continued to affect all of the French political life. The new constitutional organs were called on to function in a political world in which the forces that had killed the old order were still powerful.

Two examples come easily to the mind. The source of the discredit into which the Fourth Republic fell was the continuing war in Algeria, yet the adoption of a new Constitution, as such, did not end the Algerian war; at the best it provided better conditions for the seeking and possibly for the finding of solutions. A partly exterior event was certain to be one of the main tests of the worth of the new institutions as it had demonstrated the deficiencies of the old.

Algeria was not the only problem whose insistence on being

attended to — and solved — had been too much for the power of planning and decision of the Fourth Republic. The place of France in Europe, in the world, her relationship with her nearest neighbours, Britain and West Germany, her role in the shadow of the great powers, the United States and the Soviet Union, had been bitterly debated — ineffectively dealt with, on the whole, under the Fourth Republic (the defeat of the European Defence Community is an example of the unsatisfactory character of the decision-making machinery of the old regime). The problems of exterior relations remained no matter what new institutional adjustments were made inside France. In short, only in a secondary degree did the French Constitution concern exclusively or mainly French questions — which is one of the reasons why the outside world took a possibly too critical interest in the performance of the French political machine.

Too critical? M. Aron suggests (and I think rightly suggests) that the Fourth Republic was a less totally ineffective method of government than it was easy to damn it for being in May, 1958. A great many things were done, done well, done in time that helped to create the new France that was given new political institutions. It is not absurdly paradoxical to assert that the rapid rise in the French birth rate, the sudden "take-off" or "break-through" into the new industrial world, the cracking of the "cake of custom" that is to be seen in so much of French life, in the family, in the school, in the ambitions and tastes of the young, are more important than French constitutional changes. Indeed, they were among the potent forces imposing changes although not necessarily the kind of changes that grew out of the immediate crisis. Yet had there been no Algerian war, no General de Gaulle in the background, the contrast between the initiative and the success shown in other departments of French life, and the repeated "seizing up" of the political machine, would have been humiliating and often actively mischievous.

Yet the political machine had not prevented growth; in some sections of the economy it had actively aided it; in some it was itself an active participant in the most promising sectors of the economy (the Renault car is made by a French nationalized corporation). The French entry into the steel and coal pool, the French entry into the European common market, were not the work of the Fifth but of the Fourth Republic which was not so lacking in men of vision and courage as its enemies asserted. M. Robert Schuman and M. Pierre Mendès-France are only among the most illustrious of the political personnel whose good will, ability and character was so often frustrated by the rules of the game they had to play.

A great deal of the details of the new Constitution can only be understood in the light of the real or alleged experience of the old. The belief that governments were overthrown in order that new ministries might be formed and new ministers get their turn accounts for the exclusion of ministers from the Assembly and for the odd provision that a deputy who becomes a minister is replaced in the Assembly by a substitute who holds the seat until the next election. M. Aron is a little more confident than I am that these substitutes will accept their humble role and not set about replacing their former patrons!

Then there was nearly universal agreement that the Constitution of the Fourth Republic unduly weakened the executive and gave to the Assembly a power not merely of control,

11

but a power of initiative that it used badly. The power of the Assembly has been weakened in two ways, by the creation of a Senate with far greater powers and by the giving of greater power to the Executive, power over the life and over the day-to-day business of the Assembly. It is possible to agree with M. Aron that the nefarious effects of mere ministerial instability have been exaggerated, that if the Assembly seized up it was not due to mere cupidity or mean ambition in the members but to the fact that in the last parliament of the Fourth Republic it was difficult if not impossible to identify and organize a majority for a policy adequate to the needs of France, inside her boundaries and outside.

It was to make sure that the government of France was carried on, that French opinion and French strength should be assessed more favourably in the council of nations, that in the movement that led to the overthrow of the Fourth Republic and in the months of consultation and drafting that followed, so much thought was devoted to this question of the executive. And here we come to a difficulty that cannot be evaded and cannot be put away in some neat constitutional formula. It has more than once been said that the presidential office as it was designed by the fathers of the American Constitution owed much of its character to the fact that it was General Washington who was to be the first President. It is certain that much in the organization of the executive of the Fifth French Republic is owing to the fact that it was known that the effective head of the executive would be General de Gaulle. The effective head of the executive, not necessarily the President of the Republic. For in the discussion of the character of the new Constitution that raged in Paris (and elsewhere in France) in the autumn of 1958, it was debated whether General de Gaulle would choose to be President or to be Prime Minister. We know what choice was made and it was the natural choice, but that there could be any question of choice suggests that there is something ambiguous in the new Constitution.

There it is. It is neither a presidential constitution of the American type nor a parliamentary constitution of the English type; it is a mixture of the two. Whether it will be a happy mixture or not remains to be seen. For the moment, the question is solved. Not only did General de Gaulle choose to be President (and so stamp with name the preëminence of that institution) but the working of the Constitution has underlined presidential power. Thus the announcement of a new policy towards Algeria, a policy far bolder than any previous government had dared suggest, was a presidential act. It was not quite issued in the old monarchical form: "It is our good pleasure," but it was not in form or fact a joint effort of the President, the Prime Minister and the Assembly. All the precedents so far made have stressed the power of initiative and decision that inheres in the presidential office. And American experience suggests that what is done in the first plastic months and years hardens into effective precedent.

Yet the question is not yet decided in France. The Prime Minister must get the support of the Assembly. Will the President's choice as Prime Minister always be able to secure it? Will there not in the future be clashes between a President chosen elaborately, but remotely, by a vast electoral college representing far more than France, and an Assembly which is the direct emanation of "universal suffrage" in France? M. Aron stresses the exceptional personal powers that the President can use in his difficulties with a Prime Minister, but the chance

13

of a real deadlock is present. And when we consider the powers of the Senate, in which the rural, conservative, economically backward areas are over-represented, it is possible to wonder whether France has not been given a political engine with too many brakes rather than a dangerously stream-lined model capable of crushing all obstacles in its path. (Like M. Aron I am not alarmed by the article that gives the President exceptional powers in an emergency. The circumstances in which this power can be used will be already revolutionary or catastrophic.)

If the position of General de Gaulle underlines the truth that mere, legal formulas are not enough to describe and circumscribe the realities of power, neither are they adequate to describe and limit the popular will. That the creation of a new Constitution, a reorganization of the political and administrative machinery of France, was wanted by the mass of the people, the overwhelming "Gaullist" electoral victories of the autumn of 1958 made plain. But not only was the popular verdict one of trust in General de Gaulle much more than in his most vociferous partisans, the local elections that followed showed how tenacious the French voter was of his local liberties and powers. Faced with a break-down of state authority in May 1958, he turned to the only man who could restore authority, perhaps the only man who could avoid civil war. But the French voter was far from being a member of an hysterical mob seeking authoritative leadership, in all spheres of life, from a God-given leader. The Constitution that was produced no doubt owed much to General de Gaulle's own moderation, to his intelligently critical view of his mandate, but it also owed a great deal to the vigilance of French public opinion. France in 1958 was not Germany in 1932 or even Italy in 1923. The elements of an authoritarian solution were present, but they were not assembled and used nor did the democratic forces throw up their hands.

So it is not unnatural that the new Assembly should already show signs of wishing to expand its powers, show some resentment of the limits imposed on legislative initiative. It is not surprising that many of the leaders of the Fourth Republic, unfortunately washed out of the Assembly of the Fifth, have come back to parliamentary life *via* the Senate. It is not surprising that many cities and towns that voted overwhelmingly for General de Gaulle and inflicted on the French Communist party the most humiliating defeat of its history have yet returned their old Communist councillors and mayors to the local town halls where they have often, in the past, done useful, local service. There is no more reason to be astonished at this than to be astonished or naively indignant to the long rule of New York by Tammany. Nor is the survival of the Communist party as an effective organization in an historical and economic situation for which it is very ill adapted any more odd than the long survival of the Solid South. If French prices were lower, French supermarkets more numerous, the Communist party might decline (it is after all declining), but it would decline because like many other traditional aspects of French life it is incapable of adjusting itself to the needs of the new technological age of potential abundance. It is on the ability of the Fifth Republic to adjust itself to this age that the success or failure of its new institutions will depend.

Among the necessary adjustments is the adjustments we all have to make to the rising world of the coloured peoples, and, thanks to the boldness of General de Gaulle, what-

15

ever solution is adopted (and we must remember that it may not be an intrinsically good one) it will not be imposed or opposed by arms. And so we return to the running sore that so debilitated the Fourth Republic, the Algerian war. Since General de Gaulle's offer, the temperature has risen in France and Algeria, but so has hope. If a solution that is not ruinous to one side or the other is attained, the Fifth Republic will be justified. If it fails, as the Fourth failed, no constitutional ingenuity will do it much good — to which the converse is that if there is a real chance of a negotiated peace, none of the ambiguous articles of the Constitution are likely to be allowed to stand in the way. If the Algerian cape is doubled, then we shall be given a chance to see how the complicated machinery of the Constitution will work. And if it *does* work, the expanding France that M. Aron calls our attention to (possibly, probably, more and more merged in "Europe") will not have its energies and skills made difficult of exercise by political institutions that, without being positively nefarious, were seldom actively helpful.

The Constitution of the Fifth Republic is not an elegant or totally consistent document. Its fate will depend only in part on its text. But the text is important all the same and here we have a most acute French commentator illustrating for us not only what the Constitution formally says but what are the realities behind its formulas.

D. W. Brogan

Cambridge, October 21st, 1959

16

NOTE

Since October 1958, when the foregoing discussion took place, two events have occurred which will strongly affect the beginnings of the Fifth Republic.

General de Gaulle, elected President of the Republic, named the Prime Minister (Michel Debré), and as a result it is clear that the President will exercise a decisive influence on basic questions. The regime will be parliamentary more in law than in fact. Since the Assembly cannot change Prime Ministers without risking its own dissolution, the President can make decisions through his ministers which the Parliament will be compelled to approve. In other words, during this initial period the President of the Fifth Republic will be more powerful than the President of the United States.

Furthermore, in the elections of last November for Parliament the party that supported de Gaulle — the U.N.R. — made a remarkable showing. Although it received in the first round of elections fewer votes than the Communist party, it finally elected more than 200 deputies while the Communists ended up with only ten. The party of the classical right wing — the Independents — has some 130 deputies with whom the seventy-one Algerian deputies will join on most issues. Communists, Socialists, and Radical Socialists, who got some 40 per cent of the vote in the first round of elections, ended up with only fifty-odd of the 540 deputies (or of 470, if only the deputies from metropolitan France are counted). The majority vote, as predicted, has thus eliminated the opposition of the extreme right (Poujadists) and has reduced the Communist opposition to almost nothing. The theory espoused by the drafters of the

Constitution seems to be false — that in France, as in other countries, a majority vote would produce a majority composed of several shades of opinion.

However, I believe that the election results are deceptive. The U.N.R. is an improvised party which owes its success to the "de Gaullism" on which it campaigned. It probably cannot live beyond the exceptional circumstances that have favored it thus far; that is, the prestige of General de Gaulle. Perhaps a majority vote will regularly return a majority of the right to the Assembly because of the schism on the left between Communists and non-Communists. But this majority of the right risks division into factions.

At the moment, the power which the Independents, the U.N.R., and the Algerian deputies hold together in the Assembly seems to leave no answer to the Algerian problem except victory for the French army over the rebellion. This means prolonging the "pacification" for years to come. If the government comes to terms with the F.L.N. in Algeria, de Gaulle would probably be forced to dissolve the Assembly and let the country decide between the President and the Parliament (to which many of the deputies were elected because of their support of de Gaulle). But, even though he has steered clear of the extremists and has taken measures toward Algeria such as amnesties and cease-fire offers which those who brought him to power condemn, de Gaulle apparently does not contemplate any negotiations with the F.L.N. that would bring either immediate independence or even a national role for Algeria. In the absence of such negotiations, the war or the "pacification" will go on, and the latent opposition between de Gaulle and his supporters will remain.

R. A.

THE NEW FRENCH
CONSTITUTION

America's main interest in the new Constitution of the Fifth Republic of France is the example it may set for possible constitutions for the new states that are being created in this century. In order to explain what has been written into the new Constitution, however, I think it is necessary to see it first in the French context.

The new Constitution is based on an analysis of the defects of the previous political system in France. The main defect, according to most critics, was the instability of the Executive, and the insufficient power vested in the government.

I believe there were two forms of instability in French political life which were often confused. The first, governmental instability, I consider routine. In normal times, when there were no difficult problems to solve, the normal life of the government lasted about a year—not because everybody wanted a fundamental change but really because there was no danger of change. It was a change of government without a change of policy; it was a change of the Prime Minister, while a great number of the other ministers remained. This system could work because we had an extremely stable civil service and, in each ministry, the key civil servant played primarily a political role. He maintained continuity of policy despite the changing of ministers.

The second form of instability was completely different. It arose when we had particularly difficult problems to solve, such as the rearming of Germany in the European Defense Community, and the Algerian question. Where there is not only a multiplicity of parties, but also divisions within each party, it becomes extremely difficult to make any decisions.

Instability, therefore, reflects the inability of the Assembly and of the nation to make decisions.

This was especially true in the last two years, when we had an impossible Assembly. Of the 600 or so deputies in that Assembly, there were 200 whom I would call "out-of-bounds" deputies. By this I mean people who do not follow the rules of the game. These "out-of-bounds" deputies were the 150 Communists, and approximately thirty-five to fifty extremists of the right. As a result, there were only 400 deputies to "play the game." This meant that almost all of them had to form a majority in order to create any governmental stability.

When these deputies were profoundly divided, as they were over the Algerian question, it was impossible to find any common will and any government. In that case, the instability of the government was not only the superficial expression of the lack of party discipline and the traditional game of politics in the Assembly; it also expressed the inability of the Constitution to produce a common will and a working governmental majority in time of crisis.

Starting from this premise, everybody was convinced that France had to find a way out of the abyss. We faced the paradoxical proposition: how to find a common will in a nation where there was none. How could we find a working majority in an Assembly which had none?

Why was there no working majority based on a common will? It was admitted that the fundamental cause was the absence of disciplined parties in the French Assembly. We had too many parties, and each party was too divided and had too many opinions. Therefore, how could we find a stable government and a common will when the necessary conditions were absent?

Discussion among political scientists and politicians disclosed that there were three possible types of democratic constitutions in the twentieth century: the British type, the American type, and a third type, which is now the Constitution of the Fifth French Republic.

The British type is extremely simple. There are only two

parties, and one party has a majority. The party with the majority has discipline. So the government, which is formed by the majority party, is able to govern the nation for the term of the parliament, which is four or five years. In that case, the constitution can be extremely simple. It is enough to have the deputies elected.

The answer of the French was: "That is all very well. We should all be glad to have such a democracy, but we can't. We can't because we have no disciplined parties, and we have at least six major parties."

The second type is the American system. Here, also, there are only two parties, but they are without discipline. The key to the efficacy of the American system is the election of the President, who is the Executive by universal suffrage, for four years. Congress might differ with him on various matters, but there cannot be any question of confidence. The Executive cannot be displaced. Both the Congress and the President are there to stay, and they must come to terms if there is to be a working system.

The French had two main objections to this system. First, we tried to adopt it under the Second Republic. The result was a kind of empire. Consequently, there is a tradition of hostility to a strong President elected by universal suffrage because of the risk of a *coup d'état*. In any case, the general opinion was that the change would be too abrupt in view of the parliamentary tradition in French history.

The second objection was that the system probably works in America, not because of the Constitution, but in spite of it, since, after all, everything has been organized in the American Constitution to paralyze power. If it works, it is largely because of American tradition, custom and team spirit. Many Frenchmen were inclined to believe that the Assembly and the President in France normally would not come to terms, even if the operation of the government depended upon it. In any case, the danger would be that the cooperation achieved under the American system would be much more difficult to attain in France.

If France cannot have a stable government based on one party like the British, or a strong government based on a President elected by universal suffrage like the American, what can be done? The answer is extremely complicated. Because we can have neither strong parties nor a strong President, we must then seek a compromise. Therefore we have devised a very complicated system of relations between the President, the Prime Minister, and the Assembly. We limit the power of the Assembly in order to prevent it from becoming all-powerful and from intervening constantly in the functions of the government. In other words, the principle is separation of powers in the traditional sense of the word, but with one main difference from the British and American systems. Both Britain and America have separation of powers, but the Congress or the Parliament and the government or the President are all linked with the parties. In a sense, both systems are party systems. The new French Constitution is an effort to create a strong government based on elections but not on parties.

One of the possible uses of this system is that it might be tried in many countries in the world that are unable to create strong parties or a coherent system of parties.

❂   ❂   ❂

Now, what are the complicated provisions of the French Constitution? I think we can summarize them under three or four different headings. The first pertains to reenforcing the authority of the President of the Republic. The second defines the relation between parliament and the government. The third concerns the Constitutional Council, which is a new institution created by the Constitution of the Fifth Republic.

On paper, the President of France will be less powerful than the President of the United States. In spite of everything, the Constitution of the Fifth Republic is a parliamentary government. Proof of this is that the government is responsible to the Assembly and not to the President.

The President, whose power is defined in the second part

of the Constitution, is stronger than the President was in the Third and Fourth Republics, but he does not head the executive branch. He is the head of the state and he has certain personal power; that is, power he can use without the approval of the Prime Minister.

In the Title related to the President, many functions are enumerated. Some are powers the President can exercise with the approval of the Prime Minister; others are things he can do alone without the agreement of the Prime Minister. What he can do alone is, first, to choose the Prime Minister; second, to dissolve the Assembly; third, in certain instances, to take full powers and establish something like a dictatorship.

The oddity of this Title is Article 16, which deals with exceptional power. There was a hot discussion on this Article. It says that the President alone is responsible for judging the circumstances under which he can assume full powers. He has to consult the Constitutional Council, but he is not bound by its advice.

Of course, a legal dictatorship—one made possible by law—is surprising. But, personally, I don't believe this article is as dangerous as commonly believed, because either the President will want to become a dictator, in which case he must be ready for a *coup d'état*, or the fact that in certain exceptional circumstances he has a legal right to assume full powers will bar a *coup d'état*. If he wants to remain legal, he cannot assume full powers without justification, for, when he abandons the so-called legal dictatorship, he will be impeached. So I don't think the article is as dangerous as it was assumed in some of the discussions.

What de Gaulle had in mind is a past experience, which is always the case when you think about the future. He values the expression, "Going into the future, looking back toward the past," and the Article reflects this 1940 sentiment. In case of invasion, what can you do to avoid a break in the legal existence of the state? The answer is that the President should, in such a case, assume the role and functions of a monarch as in the past.

Besides that, when the President is not in agreement with a law voted by the Assembly, he can submit the law to a referendum without the signature of the Prime Minister. The President also names the officials, in some cases alone, in other cases after consultation with the government, for the civil and military posts of the state, state councilors, etc.

The President is elected by 80,000 to 100,000 people, including municipal councilors, members of parliament, and representatives of overseas territories. One of the characteristics of this electorate is that the rural areas will be better represented than the big towns. Some provision has been made to diminish this exaggerated view of the countryside and small villages, but still the President will be elected largely by the local councils.

The powers of the President do not make him the head of the government. According to the letter of the Constitution, he is not able to run the daily affairs of the state. But he is able to influence the government, and to apply pressure on the Assembly, by the double threat of submitting a law to a referendum or of dissolving the Assembly. In addition, the President is the head of the French Community, made up of metropolitan France and black Africa.

Of course, one of the difficulties is the relation between the President and the Prime Minister. According to the letter of the Constitution, there are two possible interpretations or evolutions. The President, when he becomes an ordinary man again, might be like the President of the Third Republic. Under the Constitution of the Third Republic, the President was conceived of as a constitutional monarch; the 1875 Constitution was drafted by an Assembly in which the majority was monarchical and hoped for the return of a king. The present Constitution goes a bit further. But there is no certainty that an ordinary President will really use the power given to him by the Constitution

Let us take only one example: the dissolution of the Assembly. It is all very well to tell the President, "You have the right to dissolve the Assembly," but his risk is enormous, because if the country returns an Assembly that again opposes the President, his position would become impossible and he would have to resign. If he is an arbiter, he cannot enter into the battle. When he enters into the battle, he ceases to be an arbiter, and, if he is beaten, he has to go.

What I have just described is exactly what happened in France in 1877. The first President of the Republic, who was not a general but a marshal, Marshal MacMahon, a monarchist, tried to use his office to influence the operation of the Constitution. He came into conflict with an Assembly which was in its majority republican. He dissolved the Assembly. The country sent back an Assembly that was still in opposition to him. The result was that MacMahon had, first, to take a Prime Minister in agreement with the Assembly and, second, to resign.

The same might happen with the President in normal times. By "normal times" I mean after the disappearance of de Gaulle. As long as de Gaulle is there, the time is not normal. The time is not normal for many reasons. When a man has full power, when he is accepted by everybody, when he is recognized by everybody as being a man of wisdom and virtue and greatness and all the rest, he can do anything, even draft the Constitution of the Fifth Republic. But this is not necessarily how it will be in the future.

Following the letter of the Constitution, the President may become only a sort of supreme adviser and supreme arbiter, and the Constitution will evolve slowly toward a more normal parliamentary form of government; or, if the President really wants to exercise power, this might produce conflict, first between him and the Prime Minister; and, second, between both of them and the Assembly.

* * *

The second aspect of the Constitution is that it has various provisions to prevent permanent aggrandizement by the Assembly, or its permanent intervention into the governing of the country. I shall note a few of these provisions.

In the last Assembly it was not necessary for a member to be present in order to vote. He could delegate his right to vote to somebody else. The result was that there could be twenty, thirty, or forty deputies in the hall and 600 votes. A regulation has been inserted into the new Constitution that says one can vote only when present.

Another provision reduces the term of the sessions. The Parliament will meet for five and a half to six months every year. According to the drafters of the Constitution this will give the government certain possibilities for action when the Parliament is not meeting.

Also, a deputy or a senator, if he becomes a minister, has to resign from his seat. This is not new for a presidential government such as America's, but it is almost without precedent in a parliamentary government, because normally the essence of parliamentary government is that a member of Parliament may become a minister. The only one other Constitution I know of in which this new French regulation is applied is the Dutch Constitution.

The question arose: When a deputy becomes a minister, who will take his seat? There were two ways of answering the question. The simplest way was to have a local election to replace him. The Minister of Justice, who had become very hostile to his fellow parliamentarians, was convinced that if there were too many elections, the election atmosphere would again impregnate the Assembly and make government operations impossible.

Therefore, it was decided that each candidate in an election should have a substitute presented at the same time as himself; there will be two candidates for each seat, and when a deputy becomes a minister his alternate takes the seat. In my view, this is the worst possible regulation. Instead of 5,000 candidates for deputies, we shall have 5,000 candidates and 5,000 alternates, and the alternate has no right to be a candidate himself the next time. Under this regulation, I believe that the majority of the ministers will still be members of Parliament whose alternates are keeping their seats in their absence.

Other regulations define the legislative process. There has been an effort to define exactly the area in which Parliament must intervene and make laws. There is an enumeration of the matters to be required by law, and they are in two different categories.

In one category, the law decides the rules in detail; in the other, the law determines only the general principles. Article 34 defines these two categories.

The law determines the rules in detail in matters concerning civil rights and fundamental guarantees accorded to citizens for the exercise of public liberties; obligations of national defense, nationality, matrimony, inheritance, and gifts; also criminal law, taxation, the elected system, public institutions, fundamental guarantees for civil servants and military personnel, and nationalization of enterprises.

Then comes a category of matters for which only the principles are determined by law. These include the general organization of national defense, free administration of local communities, education, status of property, a law pertaining to employment, unions, social security, and so on.

It is quite a responsibility to determine what, in the twentieth century, should be regulated by law and what should be regulated by what we call *décrées*, governmental or administrative regulations. The Constitution tries to discriminate clearly between the two fields.

Beyond that, the Parliament may delegate to the government the right to legislate in matters that are normally in the field of parliamentary legislation, even for the very matters enumerated in Article 34.

There is another provision for limiting instability: the government resigns only when it has been beaten. The Assembly must vote by an absolute majority in favor of a motion to censure, and this motion must be presented by at least 10 per cent of the deputies. When deputies present a motion to censure and the Assembly does not accept it, the same deputies do not have the right to propose it again during the same session. This is still another detail which has been invented to reduce the danger of permanent warfare between the Assembly and the government.

That is not all. It was thought by the drafters of the Constitution that the Assembly, elected by direct suffrage, is worse than the Senate elected by indirect suffrage. So the new Constitution restores the Senate to its position under the Constitution of the Third Republic, giving it the same power as the Assembly. This means that a law is passed only when the two chambers approve it. Since the two chambers are equal, the government has a way to paralyze the will of the Assembly with the help of the Senate.

There are cases in which a decision of the Assembly is superior to the will of the Senate, but only under one condition, which is, if the government itself decides that there should be a final vote. If the government rejects a law voted by the Assembly, but not voted by the Senate, the will of the Assembly is not done. There is a paralysis.

By all these means, then, the Assembly has been reduced to what has been considered by many commentators as a secondary function. Let us say that in the Fifth Republic the balance will be on the side of the Executive and not on the side of the Legislative. In the Fourth Republic the Assembly could do anything. In the Fifth, it has only limited initiative and power. One of the big questions is whether the limitation does not go too far.

∘ ∘ ∘

My third point is on the Constitutional Council. This Constitutional Council is necessary because of the complications of the Constitution. When you have a simple constitution like the British, you have no need of a Constitutional Council.

When you have a Federal Constitution as in America, you need a juridical body like the Supreme Court to judge in case of conflict among the various branches of government.

In our Constitution, even in so short a time, many points are already disputed. When, for example, is the Assembly going too much into the details of legislation? When is a proposal of the Assembly to be accepted or rejected? There are all sorts of possibilities of conflict inserted into the text itself. Therefore, in order to decide all cases of conflicts, there is a Constitutional Council composed of three persons chosen by the President of the Republic, three chosen by the President of the Senate, and three chosen by the President of the Assembly, plus, *ex officio*, the previous Presidents of the Republic.

This is a special sort of juridical body. It is not superior to the law voted by the Congress, as is the Supreme Court of the United States. It is only superior to all the organs of the new Constitution in the sense that in case of conflict among Senate, Assembly, Prime Minister, and President, the Constitutional Council adjudicates the issue.

The members, usually elderly, are not appointed for life, but for nine years, a length of time which affords this body considerable stability.

o o o

As a whole, the Constitution is clearly similar to those of the nineteenth century constitutional monarchies. It is a parliamentary constitution but one greatly distrustful of universal suffrage.

The National Assembly is the only body elected directly by all the people. The Senate is elected indirectly and by a limited electorate, and will tend, therefore, to be more conservative than the Assembly. The President is also elected indirectly and by a limited suffrage. The Prime Minister is not elected at all but is chosen by the President. And the Constitutional Council is not elected, but chosen by the President of the Republic, the President of the Assembly, and the President of the Senate.

This Constitution is certainly more conservative than the Constitution of the Third Republic. It is a Constitution that departs from all democratic constitutions of Western industrial societies. The key characteristic of all of these constitutions is that power is based on universal suffrage, and that it rests in the hands of those who have received a mandate from the electorate. The President of the United States is to all intents and purposes elected by the people at large. In Britain, the Prime Minister is the head of a party which has a mandate from the electorate at large.

In our system, however, there will be no equivalent of this direct mandate. Nobody knows what kind of authority the President will get from an election by the mayors and city councilors of all the villages and cities of France. Nobody knows to what extent the mayor of a small village of 200 inhabitants in the center of France is qualified to choose the President.

The people who have drafted this Constitution are, in a certain sense, good democrats. They know that outside of universal suffrage, outside of elections, there can be no legitimacy. The Constitution is an effort to combine distrust of the Assembly with the democratic principle of legitimacy. This curious combination creates a very complex machine in which the Assembly intervenes only for legislation and lets the Prime Minister and President govern the nation.

That is more or less what has been happening in the last few months and everybody is pleased. This is to be expected, because these are times of crisis in which the common man wants (a) a government that acts for him; and (b) the maintenance of all liberties. That is exactly what we have, with the special proviso that what we say or do not say does not have the slightest influence on what is done. We have complete liberty with absolute monarchy.

This curious combination—or, let us say, Roman dictatorship with full freedom—is a kind of solution. But it is a precarious one because it requires a dictator and an abnormal situation, that is, a situation in which the crises are so acute that the deputies are pleased to leave the responsibility to someone else. Acute crisis, however, is not a permanent feature of French political life, and so, for the future, some questions remain.

* * *

For the short term, the Constitution has one curious result. It makes the task of de Gaulle more difficult. That is one of the paradoxical results of this document, drafted by de Gaulle for de Gaulle. If he had taken any French Constitution of the past, he could have governed France for a few years without difficulty. But under the present Constitution, for the first time, there is a division of the executive power between the President and the Prime Minister. Under the previous Constitution, de Gaulle had only to stay as Prime Minister to govern France. In the Fifth Republic he could have remained Prime Minister. But the Prime Minister is not so decisive, and de Gaulle wanted to have an important President of the Republic. If he began the new life of the French state by retaining control as Prime Minister, the whole world would laugh. They would say, "Why all this fuss about the President of the Republic in order to have the same kind of do-nothing President?"

On the other hand, as President, he will find it extremely difficult to govern the nation because he has to name a Prime Minister. The Prime Minister, although he is an ordinary man and not de Gaulle, must govern to a certain extent.

There is one other special difficulty. De Gaulle has come to power through the help of the extreme right elements in Algeria and in France. Since coming to power, he has been fighting against the people who brought him to power because he does not belong to them, and in any case, he does not want to depend on them. An extreme right-wing majority in the next Assembly would be the normal course of events for a man brought to power by the extreme right.* As President of the Republic, with a right-wing majority in the Assembly, he has to choose a right-wing Prime Minister. At that point he may not be able to impose his own will on certain difficult questions like Algeria.

That is the immediate prospect for French constitutional life; the long-term prospect is more complicated. It may be that the French Constitution will evolve slowly toward some form of Third Republic again. The evolution, perhaps, will be characterized by a slow diminution of the function of the President, a slow reconquest by Parliament of some of the prerogatives it has lost. That would be a hopeful prospect of slow evolution toward a more parliamentary government, with better parliamentary habits than in the past.

There are also some other possibilities. The worst one is that the government, being extremely conservative and not representing the real sentiments of the French people, will clash with the Assembly. It is a pessimistic prospect.

*   *   *

An interesting aspect of the French Constitution relates to the Community. A referendum was held not only in metropolitan France, but also in Algeria and black Africa. I shall leave aside the question of Algeria for the moment because nobody there knew what the voting was all about. In black Africa the people were voting clearly for remaining inside the French Community or going out.

Guinea alone said *no*. There have been two explanations of the Guinea vote. The decisive man in this negative answer was Sékou Touré who had visited behind the Iron Curtain many times. One interpretation is that he is still a Communist or fellow traveler. I don't place much credence in this. He has been in contact with the Communists. He is certainly very

---

*See Note on page 17.

leftist. But I don't think he is now definitely committed to the Communists.

The other explanation is that there was a clash of personalities between Sékou Touré and de Gaulle during de Gaulle's tour of Africa. When de Gaulle arrived, Sékou Touré made a speech in which he said a few things that are traditional in black Africa; namely, "If we have to choose between poverty and liberty, we will choose liberty and misery rather than slavery and riches."

This is a bit of French rhetoric translated into African terms, and it is not to be taken too seriously. Actually, Sékou Touré's speech had been given to de Gaulle's man the day before it was delivered. But the text was not shown to de Gaulle, and when he heard it he was irritated. That was the beginning of the great break.

Still there might be another explanation. Of all the African territories, only one could afford to answer *no* without great risk, and that is Guinea. Why? Because there have been large investments of international money in some big industrial projects in Guinea. So even if the French take away their civil servants, even if they take away their financial help, it may be that Guinea can manage.

The Community is neither a federation nor a colonial empire. It is something in between. Each territory can become a state, but a state with limited sovereignty. They will not have armies and they will not be recognized as states by the other states, but they will have full autonomy inside their own territory, and they will be represented in an Executive Council of the Community and in a Senate of the Community. It will be something like internal autonomy, plus participation in the governing of the Community as a whole, without being fully independent.

Another feature of this Community is that its members will have permanent right to secession. That is very different from the American federation, where the right to secession was rejected by some very strong "arguments" in the last century.

The conditions for secession are clearly stated in the

Constitution. They are, first, a majority vote of the Territorial Assembly; then, a referendum in the territory; and, finally, acceptance by the French Assembly. The Community, therefore, is an effort to go from colonial status to full independence by constitutional means, possibly an effort to retain the territories inside the French Community, but without preventing them from leaving if they want to.

Already Madagascar has proclaimed that there is a state of Madagascar. Personally, I believe that there will be a slow evolution of many of these territories toward complete statehood. But it is still a question how many states there will be. For the time being, West Africa is divided into many smaller territories and there is much discussion whether they will federate among themselves or remain separated.

The problem of black Africa has largely been solved, with one exception. This is a rather fundamental qualification, that of Guinea. The answer of *no* by one territory puts the French government in an awkward position. Either we maintain very good relations with Guinea and behave toward it more or less as we do to other territories (and in that case the temptation to follow Guinea's example will be overwhelming), or we refuse to act toward Guinea as we do toward other territories. In the latter case, there is a danger of bad relations between Guinea and France. If the relations are too bad, if chaos intervenes, Guinea can become a sort of center of Communist propaganda in black Africa with considerable implications for the future.

We can hope for the success or for the failure of Guinea. If we hope for success, their example will be followed. If we hope for failure, we have trouble. My own answer, without any doubt, is that we should hope for success, but it is not yet clear what attitude the French government will take.

The government hesitates between two prospects. The people both inside and outside France who have put their money in Guinea hope for a mild policy. Some nationalists hope for a strong hand because they want Guinea to fail no matter what cost to the rest of black Africa. This is lunacy but lunacy not without precedent.

* * *

One problem has not been dealt with in the Constitution, and that is the problem of Algeria. (Algeria is, according to law, still an integral part of metropolitan France.)

This is one of the great paradoxes of the present situation. For, I think, the first time in history, France has given all its colonies the solemn right of secession. This is really commendable. It may be argued that the right of secession has been granted in order to prevent the exercise of that right, and to a certain extent it is true. Despite all the qualifications, however, it remains true that France has solemnly proclaimed that it will not keep any territory under its sovereignty if there is a real refusal by the people of that territory. Persons like myself, who favored this policy for so many years and could never get it through, ought to be thankful to those in Algeria who brought to power the only man who could engineer that policy.

But Algeria has been given less than the rest of Africa. That is the paradox. Is it possible to refuse to Algeria the right to statehood when statehood has been solemnly given to black Africa? I recognize the big difference: the one million Frenchmen in Algeria. After all, there was not the same emotional link with black Africa as there is with Algeria. It is possibly not so much the will to keep Algeria French as it is a refusal to give up the fight and lose the war. If the Falange were ready to abandon the fight, it may be that the French people would be indifferent to the independence of Algeria in a few years' time.

An opinion poll of the French nation on the problem of Algeria asked as a first question: "Is integration of Algeria into France a good thing or a bad thing?" Good thing, yes, 52 per cent; bad thing, 21 per cent; don't know, 27 per cent. So, on the whole, the French people believe that integration would be a good thing.

The second question: "Do you believe it is possible?" Answer: Yes, only 40 per cent; no, 26 per cent; don't know,

34 per cent. A good number of people, then, who believe that integration would be a good thing doubt that it is feasible.

Another question: "Many persons say that it will be necessary sooner or later to give political independence to Algeria. Are you rather in agreement with these views or rather in disagreement?"

Answer: Rather in agreement, 41 per cent. Forty-one per cent think Algerian independence sooner or later will become inevitable. Rather not in agreement, 36 per cent; without opinion, 23 per cent. The result is that only 20 per cent are really against any idea of independence, and think that integration is possible—only 20 per cent, or a fifth of the population. Some 8 per cent oppose both integration and independence; 12 per cent favor integration but think independence will be inevitable.

As you see, the French nation is not very united on the question of what to do about Algeria or about what will happen there. If you ask the people what should be done in Algeria when the nation is so profoundly divided, you get no common will. With the Constitution of the Fifth Republic, perhaps there will not be a common will, but there will be a will.

A Discussion

Question: What is the relationship of political realities and tradition to the Constitution? You said quite rightly that the American system depends upon checks and balances, but one reason it works is that the checks and balances aren't always effective, namely, we have a strong Presidency. Suppose you didn't have a strong democratic movement, right and left; suppose the Communists maintained their strength. Then you would not have the beginning of a common will and wouldn't a constitution with checks and balances be more inoperable than ours? So your final eloquent remark—about there not being a common will, but there would be a will—isn't that a question? If you haven't some kind of common will, can you get a will?

ARON: Yes, my final remark is to a certain extent the motto of the old Constitution because under it you didn't get any working majority, since there was no common will. If the French Assembly gets 200 Communists and the rest are divided, things will be the same as before. No Constitution can create something out of nothing. Still, under the new Constitution there will be a certain improvement for two reasons. First, it will be extremely difficult for the Assembly to bring down the government. There are many areas in which the Assembly will not be able to intervene and so the permanent warfare between the Assembly and the government will be eliminated.

Secondly, the composition of the last Assembly was to a large extent accidental. You can reduce the representation of extremist parties by electoral law. The new electoral law will certainly reduce the number of Communist deputies and eliminate completely the Poujadist deputies.* You will not have the same composition in the next Assembly. I should add that the composition of the last Assembly was largely the result of a mistake, because any French politician knows that in a nation where, let us say, 30 to 40 per cent of the people vote for extremist parties, you must have an electoral system which reduces their representation.

We had this under the 1951 law that permitted different parties to unite on their candidates in order to win seats. In 1956 the parties were too stupid to use this law and they produced an Assembly which prevented any government from functioning. So the next Assembly will be different, and I hope in the future we shall always have an electoral system under which the representation of the extremist parties will be reduced.

There are all kinds of pressures upon the Assembly under

*See Note on page 17.

the new Constitution, which will probably reduce the game of petty politics in the Assembly. I should say that this game in the Assembly was more or less the same as the one played in America within a party when candidates are nominated. In America, the game is not permanent. But in France, if it is played continuously in the Assembly, life becomes really difficult.

I must add one more qualification. Governmental instability was not the source of all the defects and mistakes of French political life. Many of the big mistakes were made with considerable unanimity by old governments. For example, in the 1930's the refusal to devalue the currency caused repeated crises for ten years. This mistake was committed by everybody, not only by many governments but by Parliament and by the representatives of financial interests. Nor was the war in Indochina directly the result of governmental instability. To a certain extent, I should say that French policy was too stable. By that I mean, when a mistake was committed, all governments felt obliged to repeat the same mistake.

The new Constitution comes at a time when almost all the big problems of French life have been solved with the exception of Algeria. And really, in order to solve the Algerian mess, a sort of dictatorship is necessary. Whatever one wanted to do in Algeria, it was necessary to have a new government.

Question: Is it possible to solve the problem of unity within France and governmental stability by political means? Looking at it economically, doesn't there have to be a grand transformation? One view is that the industrial revolution was never really successful in France, that you maintained peasant agriculture through your tariff policy which came about in the eighteenth century.

ARON: Late nineteenth century.

Question: You divided up the land at the time of the French Revolution.

ARON: Yes.

Question: And you maintained all the little shops of the nineteenth century. And such industry as you have in the twentieth century is not run by modern professional managers. You are still trying to perpetuate the family-type enterprise while developing a method of production that is not well suited to the family enterprise.

Couldn't it be said that until France is willing to become a modern industrial nation there can be no solution to political instability? In other words, don't you have to have a consensus about the way you operate your economy before you can have a real consensus politically?

ARON: There are two aspects to your question. One is the extent to which your description of the French economy fits the picture today, in 1958. The other is to what extent the difficulties of French political life can be explained by the economic structure. Your interpretation has been maintained by many people. I personally belong to another school.

First, what you said about the French peasant economy is true to a certain extent. Nevertheless, the process of industrialization is proceeding rapidly. Each year between 60,000 and 70,000 workers go from agriculture to the towns and industry. Secondly, the rate of growth of French industry in the last years has been extremely high. It has been about 10 per cent a year, with a per capita increase in productivity of 7 to 8 per cent over three or four years—almost too quick.

So my first comment is that, for the time being, the traditional structure of the French economy is not a paralyzing factor for economic development. My second comment is that the crisis of the French political system did not arise from internal problems. It came from the problem of the French Union. The attitude of the French people toward independence for Indochina, Tunisia, Morocco in Africa, had nothing to do with the peasant-shopkeeper issue. The real cause of this crisis was external policy.

39

When a crisis did come from economic decisions, as in the 1930's, it was not clearly related to the structure of the French economy, because the devaluation of the currency was in everybody's interest.

The actual crisis in French life for the past ten years is linked with Indochina, Tunisia, Morocco. This is fundamentally a question of what I call national conscience—of political opinion.

My third comment is that there is a lot of diversity in the French structure and in the French way of looking at things. After all, the United States of America has been even more diverse than the French nation. Any democracy has to work with a background of extreme diversity. Diversity—social, economic, psychological diversity—may be channeled into relatively disciplined parties or into political chaos. In the case of France, it was political chaos.

My own view is that the origin of French political chaos was always more political than economic. The major French quarrel of the nineteenth century, monarchy versus republic, when all economic interests could have accepted either form of government, was an ideological dispute and not a quarrel of economic interests.

If this interpretation is right—and I cannot demonstrate it—the Constitution might accomplish something.

Question: France, of all the Western countries, has had the strongest Communist party over the longest period of time. Again looking at it from an economic point of view, one can say the economic structure of France was such that the working class got the least benefit out of the industrial revolution, compared with other West European nations.

France imposed heavy tariffs to protect the farmers. The English workers got the benefit of wheat from Canada, the United States, Australia, and from all around the world. The French workers never did. In the United States, distribution became much more efficient than in France and that benefited the workers, too. There was more competition in industry and that benefited the workers.

In France, I think, if you had real competition, externally and internally, the workers would get the benefits of the industrial revolution and this would reduce their adherence to the Communist party. With 25 per cent of the vote going to the Communists, it is very difficult for democracy to operate.

So the question is whether the European market, reducing your tariffs, internal competition, and elimination of family enterprise would not do more to improve the political situation than anything else.

ARON: There is an element of truth in this theory, but I think it is largely exaggerated. For ten years wages have been higher in France than in Germany, according to any calculations. French wages are higher than the Dutch and unquestionably higher than the Italian. So the Communist attitude of the workers is not based only on the economic situation.

I admit much of what you say about the slowness of the industrial revolution, and that the workers benefit less than in some more industrialized nations. But the Germans had a large Communist party at a time when the working class did profit from the industrial revolution. The German Communist party was killed by the experience of Russia. Things are more complicated than the way you put them. The economic interpretation of the attitude of the French worker is a little too Marxist for my taste. Not just a little too Marxist, but only partly true.

The attitude of the workers might have been different if there had been a more rapid industrial revolution. But it is not explained completely by economic circumstances. Among the workers who vote for the Communists you almost always find the skilled workers; the workers in the Paris region with relatively high wages still vote Communist, or at any rate, vote Communist more than the less privileged workers do.

On your last point, that you cannot have a working democracy as long as you have a strong Communist party, I don't think that is completely true. The French Communist party has become the most conservative institution in the world. It is completely passive, completely conservative. It takes a young man with revolutionary leanings and turns him into a good bureaucrat of the Stalinist type without the slightest desire for revolution.

I am joking a bit. France's real problem with the Communist party, which has become completely bureaucratized, is to reduce its electoral representation. This can be done fairly simply.

Question: Is it not characteristic of Britain and America that, as a result of not being haunted by a feudal past, they created an economic situation which was highly conducive to consensus? Hasn't there been a kind of leveling process, a coming of satisfaction to people?

ARON: That is commonly maintained by British and American spokesmen, and I cannot refute it in a few words. If you compare Britain and France—I happen to have lived in Britain for some time—British upper-class society is much more separated from the masses than the French. The difference between Oxford English and cockney English is greater than the difference between the different types of French language.

The fact is that there is an acceptance of British upper-class society by the common man which does not exist permanently in France. This is extremely complicated to be sure, because the same Frenchman, who says he does not accept French upper-class society, may be extremely conservative and nationalistic in other ways.

Each nation has its own political temper and mood. The French mood is one of intense coherence, intense conservatism; at the same time it is violently ideological in revolutionary words. This is not a temper that makes governing very easy. Is it linked with the slowness of the industrial revolution? Maybe.

Question: It may be linked simply with the practice of sports in the British schools and the notion of the rules of the game.

ARON: There are many elements. One of the most important is this: When there is a problem to be solved in Britain, everybody says it is a difficult problem; let us try to solve it. But nobody believes that the Constitution is horrible, that the monarchy is the origin of all the evil. Each time we have a crisis in France, be it a war with Germany or Algeria, the reaction is that the Constitution is bad. It is all a matter of tradition.

Every time we had a crisis we made a new constitution. It is a sort of permanent reaction to an event. The main quality of any constitution is to be accepted, and for more than a century and a half France never had a Constitution which was generally accepted by its people. That is one more element of instability.

Question: The question is "why?" The situation you describe can be compared to what was developing in the United States in 1890, when many Americans were beginning to feel that their form of government, the Constitution if you will, was not working any more. Why did they feel that way? The lower-income groups felt it was not bringing them any adequate satisfaction and they saw no way of getting it.

ARON: This might apply to the France of the 1930's. At that time there was a paralysis of the French economy. But the last ten years have been years of very rapid recovery. During the last four years the French economy has made extraordinary progress. The dissatisfaction of the French with their regime today cannot be explained by the failure of the French economy.

Question: Except that you might say this: The French economy certainly has shown a faster rate of progress since

World War II than for almost any previous period in history and, if this goes on long enough, perhaps it will have some impact. Perhaps there can be an economic solution, if you could just keep on advancing rapidly, putting enough pressure on your entrepreneurs who have always been protected in France and who, from an American point of view, have not done a particularly good job. You say the French workers have a high standard of living. It depends upon how you look at it. They are very badly housed compared to the Germans.

ARON: Yes, but they eat better. The badly housed workers vote Communist. Even miners who have very good houses in the north and east of France often vote Communist, and they are getting higher income than the Germans on the other side of the frontier.

I have had many discussions with my friends at home and I ask: "Why are you so furious that there is a government crisis every year? It is a bit ludicrous and we should improve it, but does it really change your way of life?" Everybody said *no*.

The general dissatisfaction was not linked with economics. It was a national dissatisfaction linked with the evolution of French power in the world. In my view the dissatisfaction with the status of France in the world is much more profound than the economic dissatisfaction with housing, in spite of the fact that bad housing is one dark side of the French picture.

Question: I would follow you on this matter of France in the world if there were a party which had a political program for remedying the French position. It has not been a political issue.

ARON: It *has* been a political issue. The surprising thing is how difficult it is for the American mind to accept the fact that the loss of an empire means much more than the standard of living. We were always taught in school that decadence begins with the loss of empire. The decadence of the Roman Empire was a dark failure in history.

Question: The British are losing their empire and still keeping a smoothly functioning democratic system.

ARON: The reaction of the British to this new situation has been different from the French. The French reaction, in my view, has something to do with economics because everything has something to do with everything, but the national conscience of the French nation is at least as important as any bad economic situation and I think even more important.

Question: May I argue the economics a little bit? In France, the whole emphasis on the distribution of income is on the class shares. The peasants say, "We have to have such-and-such a share." The shopkeepers have to maintain their traditional share. It adds up to more than 100 per cent.

In the United States and Britain the distribution of income is not viewed in terms of class shares. It is in terms of the individual and the chance for him to progress. The class-share approach, it seems to me, ties back to feudalism, of people looking upon themselves as a group. The peasants are a group. The shopkeepers are a group. The economy has not been pulled together.

It seems to me that if France went the whole way toward a modern industrial system—including the destruction of the peasant class, the destruction of the shopkeepers as a class, and the increase in mobility which tends to come about in a fully developed system; the destruction of the family system, which runs enterprise more for the sake of perpetuating the family than for the profits that come from large-scale production,—you would create an economic basis more compatible with democracy.

France got messed up politically because it would not let the industrial revolution go the whole way and thus reach a kind of economic consensus behind the political consensus.

ARON: I am not quite convinced. First, the allocation of income is not a purely French problem. In the British press, you find the same kind of discussion about distribution of income. In the American press, there is discussion of the farmers' share in the American income. Even in a highly modern industrial society the question arises of the proper sharing of the general income.

On the question of shopkeepers, it is often discussed as if only France had shopkeepers. There are shopkeepers in any industrial society. I don't know if they belong to the nineteenth or twentieth century. It is not true that industry is only family business in France. All modern industry in France is corporate industry.

If the difficulty of the political system were based on the fact that the political parties represent different social classes, your point might be well taken. The fact is that you find in any party, even in the Communist party, representatives of all social groups, from the privileged people to the shopkeepers to the peasants.

In the special crisis of today, when everybody is convinced that we had the worst possible system in the world, after many years of extraordinarily rapid economic expansion, the cause could not have been fundamentally economic. It must have been something else.

Loss of empire does not mean anything to Americans because you never had the empire ideology and tradition. This is a European tradition. The British have accepted it with some reservation and where there are no important English minorities. They have not accepted it in eastern Africa where they have a small English minority and where they have tried to have multi-racial states. There we have the difficulty of the next generation.

For the time being, the logic of industrialization is fundamentally accepted in France. But there is an extremely important element to it—that the tempo must not be too rapid, because a rate of economic progress which uproots many groups in a nation increases dissatisfaction. One must not forget that France has economic expansion with a still stagnant population. When the population does not increase, increasing production and productivity is accomplished by transferring people from one job to another. This is much more painful than a transfer from one generation to another one. To a large extent the dissatisfaction today in France is not caused by the stagnation of economy but by its rapid expansion. We are experiencing the dissatisfaction of people who have to change their way of living. We have not yet arrived at the new stage where the general progress is such that the pains of transition are easily accepted.

Question: Perhaps this would be a good place for Mr. Aron to comment on the Preamble to the new Constitution, which confirmed the Preamble to the 1946 Constitution. What force has it? The way we read it, it has a distinctly Marxist ring.

ARON: The 1946 Preamble was written by an Assembly in which Communists and Socialists made up about half of the members. The 1946 Preamble is not reproduced in the 1958 Constitution, and, in any case, I don't think it had any great influence on the real working of the Constitution. The Preamble, as you know, is only a declaration of intention. It is used at times by tribunals when they have to judge cases according to the highest principles of the state. But it is not a law and its interpretation remains vague.

The 1946 Constitution was written at a time of the absolute predominance of the leftists, Socialists, and Communists; the 1958 Constitution has been drafted at a time of absolute predominance of conservative forces. Both constitutions, in my view, go too far and in opposite directions. The great danger of the 1946 Constitution was that it left all power to the Assembly. An all-powerful Assembly is satisfactory when the Assembly knows what it wants. But when there is no majority in an all-powerful Assembly, nothing results but chaos. The 1958 Constitution, on the other hand, limits the Assembly in so many ways that a leftist revision of it will become a real danger as soon as the state of urgency has disappeared. But to come back to the question, I don't think the 1946 Preamble should be taken too seriously.

Question: It is a part of the new Constitution. The 1958 Preamble says, "confirmed by the Preamble of 1946."

ARON: I can tell you why this was done. In the first draft there was no reference to the 1946 Preamble, and the opposition said, "You see what a reactionary government we have. They have destroyed all reference to social rights, to the social duty of the state, and so on." In order to disarm the leftist opposition, the Preamble was redrafted with reference to the 1946 Preamble. That is all.

Question: It is not officially a part of the present Constitution?

ARON: Yes, it is officially a part. The 1958 Preamble reaffirms the 1946 Preamble and it is marvelous that this near-Marxist Preamble should be solemnly reaffirmed by the most right-wing government.

Question: Is there any prognosis regarding the effect of this new political regime on that other old French problem, the theory of the two Frances?

ARON: It has not been relevant at all. There was a discussion only about one word of the Preamble which says that France is a *lay* Republic. It was a very hot discussion. The Catholics voted in favor of this Constitution which reaffirms the French Republic as a lay republic. It is just part of our tradition that there should be separation between church and state. It is a conservative Constitution approved by the Socialists and the bishops at the same time. So for the time being it is perfect.

Question: I should like to ask about the references to the military in the Constitution. How is that to be controlled?

ARON: There are only traditional references to the armed forces in the 1946 and the 1958 Constitutions. One is that the President of the Republic is the chief of the armed forces, which does not mean that he is the operative chief of the armies. It is a sentence retained from the monarchical tradition. The monarch was the head of the army; so is the President of the Republic. The 1958 Constitution goes a little bit further, giving some real authority to the President over the armies.

You also find in the Title related to the government that the Prime Minister has at his disposal the armies of the Republic. That is all. There is nothing about control of the armies because all the Constitutions imply the predominance of the civil power over the military.

Question: Does the Assembly determine the composition of the armed forces and their budget?

ARON: Article 34 in the fifth Title says the law determines the general principles underlying the organization of national defense. This means that the Assembly will determine the principles but the details will be reserved to the Executive.

Question: Do you know what that means?

ARON: No. The Constitution does not define the line between general principles and details. There will be an organic law which will clarify this distinction.

Question: An organic law to be passed by the Assembly and Senate?

ARON: Either it will be done by the provisional government before the meeting of the new Assembly, or it will be voted by the Parliament. Once the Constitution becomes operative, all organic laws have to be voted by the Parliament. In the interim, the government may make organic laws and, in fact, has already begun to do so.

Question: Has there been any rivalry among the different services? Has the French military expenditure been big enough?

ARON: There has been some rivalry in France, just as in any other country. A unified national defense has not progressed very much. The fight for money never went very far because since 1945 there have been the requirements of the Indochinese war and then the Algerian operations. This has been so clearly predominant over every other consideration that the fight for the division of the money was never too intense. Besides, there was never very much money.

Question: How does the treaty-making power work?

ARON: I don't think there is any change. However, in the 1946 Constitution it was clearly said that external treaties had predominance over any internal legislation.

Question: How do you ratify treaties?
ARON: As under the previous Constitution: by the Parliament.

Question: The Parliament alone?

ARON: The Parliament has two chambers, the Assembly and the Senate. Both have to ratify treaties. But in the 1946 Constitution it was stated specifically that, in case of conflict between an external treaty and the Constitution, the external treaty had predominance over the Constitution. That was the opposite of the Bricker Amendment. The predominance of external law over internal law was made absolutely clear. This is not done in the present Constitution.

People favoring European unity have the feeling that the present Constitution creates obstacles in the way of any abandonment of national sovereignty. They feel that the people who drafted the Constitution are hostile to European unity. The man who drafted the Constitution is Michel Debré,* a lawyer, who is a good friend of mine and who has been extremely hostile to European unity. However, he is, above all, a de Gaullist and if de Gaulle favors something he will accept it, too.

Question: It seems to me if Senator Bricker had written that part of the Constitution he would have written it just that way. The very things that he wanted—that a treaty should never be superior to the Constitution, that a law had to be passed by the Congress in order to make it operative, and that a treaty should be subject to judicial review—are all provided by your Constitution.

ARON: Yes. Title VI says that ratification of a treaty requires changing the Constitution. The Bricker Amendment did not go further than that, although the American problem is more complicated because of the difference between the laws of each state and Federal law. The French Constitution of 1946 stipulated that diplomatic treaties, duly ratified and published, shall have the force of law even when contrary to internal French legislation. The new one says that, if the Constitutional Council declares an international commitment to be contradictory to the Constitution, approval of the commitment requires a modification of the Constitution. It does not eliminate completely the principle of the superiority of external law, but it is more nationalistic in this respect than the 1946 Constitution.

The partisans of European integration regret this article, which makes ratification of treaties aimed at European sover-

*See Note on page 17.

eignty more difficult. At the same time it does not actually prevent them; the procedure is just more complicated.

Question: There is another very important difference. As I understand it, ratification of a treaty is enacted in exactly the same way as any other law.

ARON: Yes.

• o •

Question: Would you comment on the different kinds of law referred to in the Constitution? There is the law of the Constitution, organic law, decrees, and so on.

ARON: According to the new Constitution, there are four types of laws. The first one is the Constitution itself, which is above every other law.

The second category is the organic law. For example, there is the principle of conflict of interest between the functions of deputies and ministers in their jobs and various private and public functions. An organic law is required to determine what functions are incompatible. I cite this example because such an organic law has been drafted recently and approved by the government.

The third category is ordinary law voted by the Parliament. Such laws relate either to certain detailed questions or to the general principles of various regulations. An example of ordinary law relating to detail is fiscal law. An example of ordinary law which defines only the general principles is the organization of national defense or of education.

There is a fourth category which includes administrative rulings that have the force of law. Such administrative regulations are in turn subdivided into categories depending on the organ of government that issues the ruling and also on the relation between administrative and legislative law.

Question: Is there a sharp distinction among the various types of law, and is this new in this Constitution?

ARON: No. But it is clearer in this Constitution than in the previous one. The 1946 Constitution had constitutional law, organic law, and ordinary law; it did not give the Assembly the power to delegate the right of legislation to the government. Under the 1958 Constitution, Parliament can delegate this right of legislation, and this creates a type of law, which I have omitted, that might be called ordinance. This is a law drafted by the Executive, not voted by the Parliament. It becomes an ordinary law because it has to be approved by the Assembly, at least implicitly, although not originated by them.

Question: What sort of thing would it deal with?

ARON: Anything the Assembly would normally regulate that they might allow the Executive to legislate on for a period of time.

Question: Then there are five kinds of law.

ARON: Administrative law, which is not in the Constitution, includes many types. It may be a decree by one ministry or a decree by a council of ministers.

Question: Are these subject to judicial review by the ordinary courts?

ARON: It depends. We have two types of juridical institutions, the administrative and the ordinary. Which laws fall under which institutions has become more and more complicated with time. The new Constitution changes nothing in the French administrative system.

Question: In the debating and making of new law, the

Constitution seems to invite almost every agency of the government to participate.

ARON: The Constitution reflects the French tradition that the initiation of legislation belongs both to the government and to the Parliament. In the 1946 Constitution it was not quite the same because the Senate had less power to initiate legislation than the Assembly. In the 1958 Constitution the initiative can be taken either by the government or by the Parliament, with only one reservation, that in case of conflict the government proposal has priority in the Assembly. Joint responsibility for initiating legislation is not something new. Even in the Fourth Republic a large part of the initiative came from the government.

Question: How is law debated?

ARON: Normally it is debated in the Assembly. There is nothing new in that. What is new is that the government has the power to limit the discussion and to impose its own proposals. The government can at certain times take a text and ask the Assembly to vote the text as a whole. When the government wants to have a law passed the Assembly, it may put a question of confidence on its own text. In that case, the proposal of the government is approved if there is no motion of censure in the Assembly.

To clarify this, let's say the government wants to have a national defense measure approved by the Assembly very quickly. It puts the proposal to the Assembly and declares, after debate, that there is a question of confidence on it. If there is no motion of censure, the proposal is approved without any vote. This is an extreme form of the dominance of the government over the Assembly. Still, if the Assembly opposes the project, it can always pass a motion of censure. It cannot reject a government proposal without running the risk of a government crisis.

• ○ •

Question: I want to turn to the French Community. What would induce the members of the French Community to stay in it?

ARON: In my view, one of the great defects and dangers of decolonization is the creation of arbitrary and fictitious states; that is, territories whose frontiers were created by accident in the course of history, but which are still called states. For example, Libya has no characteristics of a state. It is not a nation; there is no unity of a nation. There are only two tribes which happen to live not too far from each other. In the decolonization movement we could imagine only one type of state—the Western type. The result was that we asked the Libyans, who had a very small population, to take on all the external characteristics of a state without the economic means of sustaining such a state.

The French have two aims. One is to maintain French sovereignty for a certain time, until these people are ready for real independence. The other is to find some intermediate solution between colonial rule and full independence.

Now why should territories stay inside the French Community? The first reason is that they get a great deal of technical help from the French expert, civil servant, and so on. Secondly, they get a certain amount of money for administrative expenses and economic development. Thirdly, they are able to manage their own affairs to a large extent without having to bear the burden of full sovereignty, which means an army and diplomacy. If they get an army and diplomacy, they will no longer receive the same amount of financial and administrative help from the French.

The fourth reason may be that if they stay inside the French Community, the educated people can divide their time between Conakry, Dakar, and Paris ... I could put it in high-sounding sentences, if you want ... But I *can* put it in more formal or diplomatic terms; that is, to be a member of a large community might be more attractive to these people than to be a member of a small African territory without much possibility of playing an important role. Just the same, I don't think this will be a strong enough reason in the future to prevent them from asking for full independence. They will want independence for their self-respect. They will want equality as a nation. They will want to be recognized as a nation and as a state. And if they want all this, they will have to leave the Community.

Title XIII in the new Constitution is called "Agreements of Association" and consists of only one Article. This Article says that the Republic or the Community may conclude agreements with states that want to associate with the Republic or with the Community in order to further their civilization. It is extremely vague, but it means that the states that have become completely independent may in some way remain linked with France. This article is intended for states like Laos, Cambodia, Tunisia or Morocco, which are fully independent but still partly French-speaking and French-administered. Tunisia and Morocco have a great number of French civil servants.

It is clear that de Gaulle's aim, if he comes to terms with the Algerian nationalists, is to conclude agreements of association with Tunisia and Morocco. Thus, there will be a new type of overseas territory. We now have possessions outside France with the status of "departments." There is the status of "territory," which is what black Africa is. There is the status of "state" inside the Community, which is what Madagascar will be in a few weeks' time. Then there is the status of "independent state" associated with the Community.

My own view is that in the course of time many states will go from their present status of member states of the Community to that of associated states. The question is whether they will advance step by step without provoking a violent psychological reaction in French public opinion. The danger of the de Gaulle dilemma—either Community or secession—is that it is a concession to the French public mood. In their present mood the French would say: "If those people want independence they can become independent, and go to hell."

The French colonial record will be judged in history by what the people do after they get independence. To tell them to go to hell if they want complete independence might be natural as a psychological reaction, but it is not very enlightened. After all, even after independence, they could remain associated with France in many ways. I think de Gaulle is much too clever not to know that as well as I do. So the only question is what sort of concession he will have to make for a while to French public opinion. The greatest difficulty will be to reconcile the psychological reaction of the colonial people with the psychological reaction of the French people.

Question: There is a tremendous drive for sovereignty now, and too often it is, as you say, artificial and for purposes of self-respect. However, the economic realities and the military realities, and possibly even the intellectual realities, require that the unit be greatly larger than these artificial states, and perhaps larger than any of us. It is this that has appealed to some of us as an experimental attempt.

ARON: I think it is a great experiment. The big question mark is how long it will last. The drive toward complete independence will not be stopped by the Community because there will always be a more extremist party in each territory saying, "We are still under colonial rule and we are exploited by the colonial power." It may last a few years; it may make the transition from colonialism to a new status orderly, peaceful, and perhaps more efficient.

Question: I suggest that the nationalists may not last indefinitely, either. They are yielding some very sterile results.

ARON: So many people in the world are interested in fostering this sterile nationalism. Still, in the present movement of nationalism, there are certain authentic trends that must be accepted as necessary. There is also the resentment and the exploitation of grievances, real or fictitious. As always in human history, it is a mixture of good and evil.

Question: It was explained to us that the trouble with Tunisia is that it's too small. It does not have within it the resources of a viable state. The question is whether they move in the direction of a United Arab Republic or in some other direction, since it appears from the nature of their state, their geography, their resources, that they cannot exist alone.

ARON: After all, Africa was never a nation in the Western sense of the word. There have been times when it has had the beginnings of empires. They were always created by armed force and maintained by armed forces. Now we are trying to create states and nations. All of them are so heterogeneous and most of them are so small that their capacity to exist under democratic freedom is always obscure and precarious. So the Community might be a transitional state. I do not believe that we can stop for all time the drive toward full independence. There may be different types of states, and it may be, if the French Government is flexible enough, that the people will go from the Community to association without noticing the difference, which would be ideal.

The key to the future of French relations with Africa is Algeria. Whatever happens in black Africa will not be decisive for the short-term period of twenty or twenty-five years. There is no strong emotion in France about black Africa. These people have no great religious or cultural tradition to put them in conflict with Europe. The great difficulty is North Africa, where we are facing a part of the Moslem world. In spite of all the differences between the Moslems of the Middle East, Asia, and North Africa, they are all part of the Moslem world. If the French leave North Africa completely, it is probable that North Africa will become a part of the Moslem world, including the Middle East. This would have very dangerous consequences for Europe and the whole Western world.

On the other hand, if conflict between France and Algerian

nationalism goes on, even if the French Army gets the upper hand, the consequences will be bad because of the hostility of the rest of the Moslem world. So the big question is, will there be any agreement between the three North African states and France? Without this agreement there is no hope, even if the French Army wins. It will require some sort of conciliation between Algerian nationalism and France. It appears immensely difficult, but it is on that issue that de Gaulle will be judged in the long run. If he can achieve an agreement, I believe it will be the political masterpiece of the century. Six months ago I would have said that there is no prospect of conciliation. Today I say there is a ray of hope. No more.

Question: Would it be true to say that the only possibility is that de Gaulle would dissemble—in order to reduce the extremists in Algeria he has surreptitiously or by gentleman's agreement promised the Algerians ultimate independence, a thing he cannot say in France?

ARON: He cannot offer independence to the Algerians or even promise them ultimate independence. But he might give them such a political status in the short run that they will have the prospect of ultimate independence if they play the game. If he offers them autonomy with universal franchise, he is implicitly proposing ultimate independence. The question is whether the F.L.N. will settle for what is only an implicit promise. The maximum he can give is an implicit promise, nothing explicit.

Question: It seems to me that these problems are rather artificial in the context of France and Algeria, because as soon as the dust settles in France, the larger problems—the external problems of Western Europe vis-à-vis the growing power of Russia, the military problems—will begin to make their pressure felt. I do not see what there is in the Constitution to provide for those eventualities which cannot be very distant for the whole system to survive.

North Africa is clearly essential for the defense not only of France but of all Europe, the flanks of Europe. You cannot think of a viable Western Europe with North Africa in any way hostile. I don't know why the other countries of Western Europe don't see this—the military understand it perfectly well. Somehow or other there has to be a combination. There can be no question of permitting North Africa to go into the general Arab world and under strong Communist influence, if the safety of Europe is to be considered seriously.

It is difficult for me to understand why, with General de Gaulle so experienced, they have not envisioned making North Africa another country bound somehow or other into the Western European system. Certainly you cannot let them go their own way if the way is the way of Egypt.

ARON: Yes, that is all very true and reasonable. I agree with every word, but with one qualification; that is, that the Western world has become used to accepting abstract political principles without reference to opportunity or military necessity. I don't see a single Western government capable of limiting the independence of another people, even if it is a military necessity. I don't see that the United States has ever said, "We will keep Panama with armed force if need be, because it is necessary for the defense of North America." The justification of a political move merely because of its military expediency has disappeared from our hypocritical world. This is, unfortunately, one of the key factors of the situation.

With regard to North Africa specifically, Tunisia wanted independence, or a certain number of people in Tunisia wanted independence. In Morocco, a certain number of people wanted independence. So, according to our principles and the anti-colonial emotions of the Western world, we gave independence to Tunisia and Morocco. We couldn't put military expediency ahead of principle. In Algeria there are 9,000,000 Moslems and 1,000,000 French. If we say, "We keep Algeria because we need it for military reasons," we will be alone. Not a single Western government will support us. The American government is divided. On one side are the military people. But on the other side the State Department, or in any case the Moslem Desk of the State Department, says, "My God, if we come into conflict with the Moslems, we will have the whole Moslem world against us. These damn Frenchmen and their colonialism, what can we do about them?"

Britain says, "It would be a pity if we had enemies in North Africa, but what else can you expect from the French?" In Germany: "We had the good luck to have these damn French and British take away our colonies, so we are the only people in Europe without colonial representation. It makes it possible for us to have all sorts of trade relations with the Middle East and Asia. For God's sake, let these damn Frenchmen find a way out." In Italy: "Our greatest victory was the loss of our colonies after the war. Between the two wars we kept asking ourselves why we had so much trouble with our economy. We found the answer. We spent too much on the colonies. Now, by good chance, we have no colonies. There are all sorts of privileges in relation to the colored people; let us retain these privileges."

The European countries, each one being a sovereign and national state, have a short-term view of their own interest. Certainly it would help if the French government could draft a policy acceptable to the ideologies of the Western world while maintaining fundamental military security. That would be something like telling the Algerians, "Of course, in the long run we are ready to accept your right to independence, but we need a minimum security guarantee." Not only the French but the whole NATO Alliance should seek the maintenance of military bases, and this could be negotiated. But the French will say, "We are grown-up people. We will deal alone with our difficult affairs. If we offer a common policy to Bonn, London, Rome and Washington, each will have a different view, and no common policy will result. Therefore, we run the danger of either a very long war or of losing everything."

You are perfectly right that if we take a global view it is

absurd for the Europeans not to be conscious of what is at stake in North Africa. But if we take not a historical view but a political view, the difficulties are enormous in trying to do what reason should demand.

Question: On one side there is danger of autonomy for nations that can't be nations; on the other side, the failure to do justice to the ethnic and cultural facts that make nations. Algeria has been a potential nation embodied in metropolitan France. This is the mistake you now have to correct; is that right?

ARON: Yes. If we look at the history of France in Algeria, it must be said that nobody knew at the start why we went into Algeria at all. We went there in 1830 for a diplomatic incident or accident. We dispatched an army but a large part of French opinion was never much in favor of the conquest. Marshal Bugeaud, who was the soldier responsible for the conquest, told the French Assembly in 1830 that the most reasonable thing to do would be to abandon Algeria altogether. But, he added, unfortunately the government in Paris is too weak to do that. Since it was too weak to abandon Algeria, it had to conquer it completely.

Today we are in the same situation. The French government is too weak to abandon Algeria and so we have to conquer it again. We have been doing it for four years and it may go on for some time still. Now what do we have in Algeria? We have a small French society with 1,000,000 Frenchmen and between 1,000,000 and 2,000,000 Moslems integrated into French society, and the rest—7,000,000 Moslems —living more or less in traditional conditions outside of the French civilization. This is a diabolical situation, extremely difficult to maintain by force, even more difficult to abandon. If we try to integrate the rest of the population into French society, it will cost an enormous amount of money and bring dubious results, because if these people become good Frenchmen they will ask for independence in the name of French democratic ideology. The most nationalistic Algerians are the French-educated.

It will go on this way. In Asia the British had only an indirect hold. There was a small upper class of civil servants and administrators. They created administrators among the natives, and so, when the time came, they could deliver the government to the political party fighting for independence. In North Africa, Tunisia and Morocco got French capital, French experts, French administration. Then we granted them independence, and deterioration in the economic situation was inevitable.

As for Algeria, the French minority doesn't want to be treated like the French minorities in Tunisia and Morocco, and so we have to stick. How we can find any sort of reconciliation with the Moslem nationalists, even if we join with all other Europeans and work together, is an almost insoluble problem.

* * *

Question: Is it possible that a Constitution, being a basic law, will develop a political life and a political way of thought and even an economy?

ARON: Yes. I should say that even if in the short term the present Constitution improves the functioning of the government, for a longer term it is a dangerous device. It will not work for a modern system; it will restore the past system.

If we say that the normal modern system requires a system of coherent parties, the present Constitution will make this almost impossible. An example of this is the return to the one-man constituency. The election by list encouraged strong parties. But the present system, where each man is elected in his own name, prevents the development of strong parties. The probable effect of the present Constitution will be to maintain the multiplicity of very loosely organized parties. It will not work in the direction of a system of coherent parties. It will work in the direction of restoring a Parliament of personalities and not of parties. If you have a Parliament of personalities, you must have all sorts of regulations, giving the Executive more power and the Parliament less.

This Constitution is an effort to apply the mechanism of constitutional monarchy to overcome the chaos of a system without strong parties. That is more or less its main purpose. Is the system of strongly organized parties, as it exists in Britain, America, the Scandinavian countries, Benelux, Germany, even Italy, necessary for a modern democracy? Or can there be another type without parties? I cannot give an answer. But I find it difficult to believe that in a French industrial society, when two-thirds of the population will be living in big cities, we can still have a system of representation by personality without party organization.

Question: If you anticipate a breakdown in this, or some dissatisfaction with it in ten years, what would you suggest for a new Constitution?

ARON: If the key to a functioning democracy is a system of parties, the essential thing would be to try to reorganize the parties. Personally, I hope that in this intermediate phase there will be some effort toward regrouping the parties, but the electoral law is not very favorable to that.

Question: Looking ahead ten years, and not just for France but generally, it may be that the tendency will be toward a new system such as now exists in Austria, where you have a kind of negotiated settlement between the major economic groups. Holland has done this pretty well, too. It used to be called the Foundation of Labor, a kind of negotiated settlement between the major interest groups, over who gets what, and how things are going to be operated to maintain certain basic privileges for both groups. Each of the major groups has a kind of veto over the other group, and the open battle of parties which we have seen in the past—whether in a two-party system or a multi-party system—is more or less at an end.

Maybe there will be parties, but they won't really fight about much of anything. They will work toward a negotiated settlement. If the logic of industrialization is that you have to have consensus in order to make this very interdependent economic system work, and if the interdependent economic system does not work, I would argue that the interdependent political system does not work. You may have your parties, but behind the scenes they are going to negotiate the basic issues.

ARON: Yes, I am in fundamental agreement with you. I have written that the industrial society is developing a party system where there is almost no stake in the discussion. Only secondary questions are discussed in the political party. It is striking that the great political battles of the last twelve years in all countries of the West have been largely on questions of foreign policy and not of internal policy. The only big political battle in Britain was over Suez. In America, the big quarrel was about communism, which was not completely an internal question. There was a terrible battle about MacArthur, Korea, the conduct of foreign policy, but not about internal affairs as long as there was sufficient prosperity.

Despite appearances, it is exactly the same in France, if you leave aside the period of extreme inflation. From the time France reached relative stability—let us say since 1952—there have been very few strikes. There has been fundamental agreement between the trade unions and the managers, and even fundamental agreement among the trade unions, the managers, and the peasants. There was only a marginal conflict over the price of wheat in relation to the level of wages. France has had fundamentally the same evolution as all industrial societies whose interdependence is such that any fundamental battle among the different groups becomes absurd.

But some questions remain, which are outside this implicit agreement. These are the questions of foreign policy. In America—MacArthur and the Korean War, and perhaps the China policy. In Britain, although there was almost no discussion about abandoning India because it was seen to be inevitable, there was less unanimity about the Middle East and a profound division about Suez. This was overcome because the British are a reasonable and pragmatic people and saw that it did not work in Suez and that they had to find another way. The French, being of a different temper, said it should have worked if the Americans had been less stupid.

Question: May not the problem of modern society be one of the benevolent monarch—and I don't know what the term for this would be—an aristocracy or plutocracy? You are going to have at the top of society the big trade union leaders, the big leaders of industry. Perhaps this is a benevolent oligarchy. The problem is how to keep it benevolent and limited. This is a problem of modern industrial society, forgetting the two-party system and all the rest of that. How do you have a benevolent and limited economic oligarchy running an industrial society? In a complicated, intricate industrial society, everybody is concerned about keeping the machinery running. You can't have strikes, you can't have divisive conflicts. How do you do it?

ARON: In the case of France, there is another phenomenon. We in France have the curious habit of going from extreme anonymity to extreme personal power. When the urgency is great, we give full power to the man who happens to be there. I say absolute monarchy because I read the expression in *The New York Times* and I think the French were rather pleased with it. The French are not averse to a strong power under three conditions.

First, the man who has full power must say that he is the expression of the people, so the people should not have the impression that they are governed by an external power. Secondly, the absolute monarch must be benevolent. Thirdly, he must not interfere with their normal living. The fact that the Parliament disappeared for a few months was therefore not much of a shock to the French, especially since they knew that it would come back.

It seems to me that a certain decadence of the parliamentary institution is inevitable. This is linked with the evolution of industrial society. It has become extremely difficult to discuss the fundamental problems of an industrial society in a Parliament where a great number of elected people really have no competence.

I agree that the tendency is to find a benevolent oligarchy, but I have one reservation. The political institution must be of a type that will achieve two results. First, it must prevent the expansion of totalitarian rule; that is, it must protect public liberties in a very efficient manner. Second, it must give the impression to the common man that he has some participation in the machinery of government and decision. The latter result is most difficult. It is all very well to say that society has become too complicated and the common man has to be governed from the outside. But he wants to feel that he chose the people who are governing him. This condition is not so easy to meet.

Question: I should put a different name on what has been called the industrial oligarchy and call it the benevolent bureaucracy. I think the kind of issues that are discussed in parliaments and congresses seem to be declining in relevance and importance, and the bureaucracy—the civil service—continues to grow. You have suggested that most of the important governmental acts were taken by the French civil service, which you also suggest has not been changed by the changes in government.

ARON: Not at all.

Question: And the discussions were irrelevant to the operation of government very often. Then what difference does the new Constitution make?

67

ARON: There are two things: First, the previous Constitution, or the way it was administered, made the government so weak that it was often a slave of special pressure groups. The drafters of the new Constitution hope that the government will have stronger powers of resistance to the pressure groups.

The second thing is that France still has some foreign policy decisions to make. We are waiting for the day when politics will consist only of the administration of industrial society. Meanwhile, we are immersed in a sea of conflicting interests, and the government has to make decisions about Africa—Algeria, Tunisia, Morocco, and so on. It is hoped that the next government will be able to follow a given policy even if the majority of the nation does not agree with it and that the majority of the Assembly will accept a decision which it itself would have been unable to make.

Question: So the Parliament becomes a kind of system for getting acquiescence to the decisions that are forced by circumstances on the government?

ARON: Parliament remains necessary (a) to protect liberty; (b) to give the people the occasional chance of expressing their preferences; and (c) to give the common man the impression that the government is not taking this decision alone but that it has to be approved by the representatives of the people.

* * * *

Question: Let us take the agitation leading up to the present Constitution, which seemed to center around the idea of a strong President of the Republic. Then you get a Constitution generated by a strong President of the Republic, and at the same time you maintain a parliamentary government. The first thing is that the President of the Republic has to choose a Prime Minister. Under the parliamentary system he cannot choose a Prime Minister or, at any rate, he can do so only under the most extraordinary circumstances, when there is no majority in Parliament. There is nothing inherent in the French Constitution that prevents this strong President of the Republic from becoming about as strong as the Queen of England under normal conditions; is that correct?

ARON: Nothing at all. In the discussion about the Constitution, the striking fact was that, before it was drafted, people like Debré said it is absolutely necessary to have a very strong President. And after it was drafted, its opponents said this is no longer a parliamentarian government; the President is too strong. Then Debré went on the other side and said, "This Constitution sets up a purely parliamentary government. Essential power is in the hands of the Prime Minister." In that case, where is the big change from the past? Nobody knows exactly what the President can do. The best proof of that is that so many people are saying, "But when de Gaulle is no longer Prime Minister and becomes President, will he be able to act?"

This still leaves the other element, which is the limitation of the powers of the Assembly. This, in my view, is much more important than the question of the President. The key to the new Constitution is the limitation of the Parliament.

Question: Are there no forces released by the Constitution that will tend toward the reduction of the number of parties? You indicated that you expected a multiplicity of parties to continue, perhaps even to increase. If the members of Parliament are to assert themselves against the Executive, might it not occur to them that coalescence and union would promote their strength and that parties that have hitherto been fractions or splinters might seek to become a countervailing power through union?

ARON: What are the main factors favoring strong parties in any nation? An important one is electoral necessity. In

69

order to get votes you must stand together, and you need strong parties inside the Assembly. In America, the parties are not disciplined in the Congress. They exist mainly because they are vote-getting machines. But in the new French Constitution nothing is done to make the vote-getting machines necessary. Under the new electoral law, it will be the man who is elected rather than the representative of a party, so there is no clear influence toward reenforcing the parties.

It may be that the deputies will feel the necessity of discipline in the Assembly, but it is not very clear why, because parliamentary work is so organized, under the new Constitution, as to favor individual activity rather than action by well-organized parties. It is difficult to predict. It may be that there will be in time another election law. For the present we don't see very clearly where the impulse to have strong parties would come from.

Question: Mr. Aron, you said several times that your major disappointment with the new Constitution is the limitation on the Assembly.

ARON: No. The exaggeration of the limitation. I was very much in favor of putting certain limits to the activity of the Parliament, but you should not go too far. If you go too far, you discredit the institution itself. If a constitution shows too clearly that there is no confidence in the ability of the representatives to act reasonably, everybody will feel, why accept this institution, if the people elected are so stupid?

Every conceivable limitation is put on the activity of the one Assembly which is directly elected by the people. To have a principle of legitimacy which is denied by the way in which public institutions are organized seems to me to be dangerous. Furthermore, it is difficult to conceive that the politicians will accept permanently all these limitations. I am afraid that the battle for revision will come very soon. That is my objection.

Question: If you were writing a Constitution today, would you say something about labor unions and about organizations of economic power in some way? We have the impression that business corporations, in the form of cartels and so forth, have a sort of special relationship to the rest of society.

ARON: One of the long-standing objections to the functioning of our institutions was the weakness of government in relation to pressure groups. It was said that the big business lobby was too strong and the French government too weak. There was never any tendency to write these pressure groups into the Constitution because nobody knew exactly what to do. These groups exist. They exist everywhere, and they are an important feature of modern society. On the other hand, they have no place in the traditional organization of legal parties. The Constitution recognizes the citizens, the elected body, but ignores the interest groups. What is there to say about them? That they have the right to exist? They exist. The right to exist is based on the right to organize groups.

The idea behind the Constitution seems to be that if the government is sufficiently divorced from the Assembly it will be stronger against the pressure groups.

Question: I take it from what you have said about the parties that you believe the structure within which the parties operate has a very substantial influence on their effectiveness.

ARON: Yes.

Question: What bothers me is that I can't see in American or French history why a lot of parties developed in one society and only two ever came to have great importance in America.

ARON: The great diversity of denominations, sects and parties in America which did not develop into many parties on the federal level has been discussed many times, as you

71

know. There are many reasons for this. I think one of the main ones is the direct election of the President. This makes it extremely difficult for splinter parties to play an important role on the federal scene. You have the election of the head of the executive by universal suffrage. Even if you had many parties, it wouldn't change the fact that there is one man in a position to act. One of our special problems was that we asked the parties to create a majority able to act in common. That is something fundamentally different from your own case. Logically, we should have tried the presidential regime because normally you counteract the multiplicity of parties by securing the head of the executive through universal suffrage. But for various reasons, among them traditional reasons, the presidential system was rejected, so we had to have this complicated and combined system.

Question: There is no chance that the 80,000 or 100,000 people who are going to elect the President will tend to form into a few parties?

ARON: No, I don't think so, because these people are local mayors and city councilors. They would not even meet. Each one will vote in his own department.

APPENDIX

Preamble to the 1946 Constitution

Text of the New Constitution

PREAMBLE TO THE 1946 CONSTITUTION

On the morrow of the victory of the free peoples over the regimes that attempted to enslave and degrade the human person, the French people proclaim once more that every human being, without distinction of race, religion, or belief, possesses inalienable and sacred rights. It solemnly reaffirms the rights and freedoms of man and of the citizen consecrated by the Declaration of Rights of 1789 and the fundamental principles recognized by the laws of the Republic.

It further proclaims as most vital in our time the following political, economic and social principles:

The law guarantees to women rights with men in all domains.

Anyone persecuted because of his activities in the cause of freedom has the right of asylum within the territories of the Republic.

Everyone has the duty to work and the right to obtain employment. No one may suffer in his work or his employment because of his origin, his opinions, or his beliefs.

Everyone may defend his rights and interests by trade-union action and may join the union of his choice.

The right to strike may be exercised within the framework of the laws that govern it.

Every worker through his delegates may participate in collective bargaining to determine working conditions, as well as in the management of business.

All property and all enterprises that now have or subsequently shall have the character of a national public service or a monopoly in fact must become the property of the community.

The nation ensures to the individual and the family the conditions necessary to their development.

It guarantees to all, and notably to the child, the mother, and the aged worker, health protection, material security, rest, and leisure. Every human being who, because of his age, his physical or mental condition, or because of the economic situation, finds himself unable to work, has the right to obtain from the community the means to lead a decent existence.

The nation proclaims the solidarity and equality of all Frenchmen with regard to the burdens resulting from national disasters.

The nation guarantees equal access of children and adults to education, professional training, and culture. The establishment of free, secular public education on all levels is a duty of the state.

The French Republic, faithful to its traditions, abides by the rules of international law. It will not undertake wars of conquest and will never use its arms against the freedom of any people.

On condition of reciprocity, France accepts the limitations of sovereignty necessary to the organization and defense of peace.

France forms with the people of its overseas territories a union based upon equality of rights and duties without distinction of race or religion.

The French Union is composed of nations and peoples who wish to place in common or co-ordinate their resources and their efforts in order to develop their civilization, increase their well-being, and ensure their security.

Faithful to her traditional mission, France proposes to guide the peoples for whom she has assumed responsibility toward freedom to govern themselves and democratically to manage their own affairs; putting aside any system of colonization based upon arbitrary power, she guarantees to all equal access to public office and the individual or collective exercise of the rights and liberties proclaimed or confirmed above.

Text provided by French Embassy Press and Information Division.

TEXT OF THE
NEW CONSTITUTION

PREAMBLE

The French people hereby solemnly proclaims its attachment to the Rights of Man and the principles of national sovereignty as defined by the Declaration of 1789, reaffirmed and complemented by the Preamble of the Constitution of 1946.

By virtue of these principles and that of the free determination of peoples, the Republic hereby offers to the Overseas Territories that express the desire to adhere to them, new institutions based on the common ideal of liberty, equality and fraternity and conceived with a view to their democratic evolution.

ARTICLE 1

The Republic and the peoples of the Overseas Territories who, by an act of free determination, adopt the present Constitution thereby institute a Community.

The Community shall be based on the equality and the solidarity of the peoples composing it.

Title I

ON SOVEREIGNTY

ARTICLE 2

France is a Republic, indivisible, secular, democratic and social. It shall ensure the equality of all citizens before the law, without distinction of origin, race or religion. It shall respect all beliefs.

The national emblem is the tricolor flag, blue, white and red.

The national anthem is the "Marseillaise."

The motto of the Republic is "Liberty, Equality, Fraternity."

Its principle is government of the people, by the people and for the people.

ARTICLE 3

National sovereignty belongs to the people, which shall exercise this sovereignty through its representatives and by means of referendums.

No section of the people, nor any individual, may attribute to themselves or himself the exercise thereof.

Suffrage may be direct or indirect under the conditions stipulated by the Constitution. It shall always be universal, equal and secret.

All French citizens of both sexes who have reached their majority and who enjoy civil and political rights may vote under the conditions to be determined by law.

ARTICLE 4

Political parties and groups shall be instrumental in the expression of the suffrage. They shall be formed freely and shall carry on their activities freely. They must respect the principles of national sovereignty and democracy.

Title II

THE PRESIDENT OF
THE REPUBLIC

ARTICLE 5

The President of the Republic shall see that the Constitution is respected. He shall ensure, by his arbitration, the regular functioning of the governmental authorities, as well as the continuance of the State.

He shall be the guarantor of national independence, of the integrity of the territory, and of respect for Community agreements and treaties.

ARTICLE 6

The President of the Republic shall be elected for seven years by an electoral college comprising the members of Parliament, of the General Councils and of the Assemblies of the Overseas Territories, as well as the elected representatives of the municipal councils.

These representatives shall be:

—the mayor for communes of fewer than 1,000 inhabitants;

—the mayor and the first deputy mayor for communes of from 1,000 to 2,000 inhabitants;

—the mayor, first deputy mayor and a municipal councillor chosen according to the order in which he appears on the council list for communes of from 2,001 to 2,500 inhabitants;

—the mayor and the first two deputy mayors for communes of from 2,501 to 3,000 inhabitants;

—the mayor, the first two deputy mayors and three municipal

councillors chosen according to the order in which they appear on the council list for communes of from 3,001 to 6,000 inhabitants;

—the mayor, the first two deputy mayors and six municipal councillors chosen according to the order in which they appear on the council list for communes of from 6,001 to 9,000 inhabitants;

—all the municipal councillors for communes of more than 9,000 inhabitants;

—in addition, for communes of more than 30,000 inhabitants, delegates appointed by the municipal council in the ratio of one delegate for every 1,000 inhabitants above 30,000.

In the Overseas Territories of the Republic, the elected representatives of the councils of the administrative units shall also form part of the electoral college under the conditions to be determined by an organic law.

The participation of member States of the Community in the electoral college for the President of the Republic shall be determined by agreement between the Republic and the member States of the Community.

The procedures implementing the present article shall be determined by an organic law.

ARTICLE 7

The President of the Republic shall be elected by an absolute majority on the first ballot. If this is not obtained, the President of the Republic shall be elected on a second ballot by a relative majority.

The voting shall begin at the summons of the Government.

The election of the new President shall take place twenty days at the least and fifty days at the most before the expiration of the powers of the President in office.

In the event that the Presidency of the Republic has been vacated, for any cause whatsoever, or impeded in its functioning as officially noted by the Constitutional Council, to which the matter has been referred by the Government, and which shall rule by an absolute majority of its members, the functions of the President of the Republic, with the exception of those provided for by Articles 11 and 12 below, shall be temporarily exercised by the President of the Senate. In the case of a vacancy, or when the impediment is declared definitive by the Constitutional Council, the voting for the election of a new President shall take place, except in case of *force majeure* officially noted by the Constitutional Council, twenty days at the least and fifty days at the most after the beginning of the vacancy or the declaration of the definitive character of the impediment.

ARTICLE 8

The President of the Republic shall appoint the Premier. He shall terminate the functions of the Premier when the latter presents the resignation of the Government.

On the proposal of the Premier, he shall appoint the other members of the Government and shall terminate their functions.

ARTICLE 9

The President of the Republic shall preside over the Council of Ministers.

ARTICLE 10

The President of the Republic shall promulgate the laws within fifteen days following the transmission to the Government of the finally adopted law.

He may, before the expiration of this time limit, ask Parliament for a reconsideration of the law or of certain of its articles. This reconsideration may not be refused.

ARTICLE 11

The President of the Republic, on the proposal of the Government during [Parliamentary] sessions, or on joint motion of the two assemblies, published in the *Journal Officiel*, may submit to a referendum any bill dealing with the organization of the governmental authorities, entailing approval of a Community agreement, or providing for authorization to ratify a treaty that, without being contrary to the Constitution, might affect the functioning of [existing] institutions.

When the referendum decides in favor of the bill, the President of the Republic shall promulgate it within the time limit stipulated in the preceding article.

ARTICLE 12

The President of the Republic may, after consultation with the Premier and the Presidents of the assemblies, declare the dissolution of the National Assembly.

General elections shall take place twenty days at the least and forty days at the most after the dissolution.

The National Assembly shall convene by right on the second Thursday following its election. If this meeting takes place between the periods provided for ordinary sessions, a session shall, by right, be held for a fifteen-day period.

There may be no further dissolution within a year following these elections.

ARTICLE 13

The President of the Republic shall sign the ordinances and decrees decided upon in the Council of Ministers.

He shall make appointments to the civil and military posts of the State.

Councillors of State, the Grand Chancellor of the Legion of Honor, Ambassadors and envoys extraordinary, Master Councillors of the Audit Office, prefects, representatives of the Government in the Overseas Territories, general officers, rectors of academies [regional divisions of the public educational system] and directors of central administrations shall be appointed in meetings of the Council of Ministers.

An organic law shall determine the other posts to be filled in meetings of the Council of Ministers, as well as the conditions under which the power of the President of the Republic to make appointments to office may be delegated by him and exercised in his name.

ARTICLE 14

The President of the Republic shall accredit Ambassadors and envoys extraordinary to foreign powers; foreign Ambassadors and envoys extraordinary shall be accredited to him.

ARTICLE 15

The President of the Republic shall be commander of the armed forces. He shall preside over the higher councils and committees of national defense.

ARTICLE 16

When the institutions of the Republic, the independence of the nation, the integrity of its territory or the fulfillment of its international commitments are threatened in a grave and immediate manner and when the regular functioning of the constitutional governmental authorities is interrupted, the President of the Republic shall take the measures commanded by these circumstances, after official consultation with the Premier, the Presidents of the assemblies and the Constitutional Council.

He shall inform the nation of these measures in a message.

These measures must be prompted by the desire to ensure to the constitutional governmental authorities, in the shortest possible time, the means of fulfilling their assigned functions. The Constitutional Council shall be consulted with regard to such measures.

Parliament shall meet by right.

The National Assembly may not be dissolved during the exercise of emergency powers [by the President].

ARTICLE 17

The President of the Republic shall have the right of pardon.

ARTICLE 18

The President of the Republic shall communicate with the two assemblies of Parliament by means of messages, which he shall cause to be read, and which shall not be followed by any debate.

Between sessions, Parliament shall be convened especially for this purpose.

ARTICLE 19

The acts of the President of the Republic, other than those provided for under Articles 8 (first paragraph), 11, 12, 16, 18, 54, 56 and 61, shall be countersigned by the Premier and, should circumstances so require, by the appropriate ministers.

Title III

THE GOVERNMENT

ARTICLE 20

The Government shall determine and direct the policy of the nation.

It shall have at its disposal the administration and the armed forces.

It shall be responsible to Parliament under the conditions and according to the procedures stipulated in Articles 49 and 50.

ARTICLE 21

The Premier shall direct the operation of the Government. He shall be responsible for national defense. He shall ensure the execution of the laws. Subject to the provisions of Article 13, he shall have regulatory powers and shall make appointments to civil and military posts.

He may delegate certain of his powers to the ministers.

He shall replace, should the occasion arise, the President of the Republic as chairman of the councils and committees provided for under Article 15.

He may, in exceptional instances, replace him as chairman of a meeting of the Council of Ministers by virtue of an explicit delegation and for a specific agenda.

ARTICLE 22

The acts of the Premier shall be countersigned, when circumstances so require, by the ministers responsible for their execution.

ARTICLE 23

The office of member of the Government shall be incompatible with the exercise of any Parliamentary mandate, with the holding of any office at the national level in business, professional or labor organizations, and with any public employment or professional activity.

An organic law shall determine the conditions under which the holders of such mandates, functions or employments shall be replaced.

The replacement of members of Parliament shall take place in accordance with the provisions of Article 25.

Title IV

THE PARLIAMENT

ARTICLE 24

The Parliament shall comprise the National Assembly and the Senate.

The deputies to the National Assembly shall be elected by direct suffrage.

The Senate shall be elected by indirect suffrage. It shall ensure the representation of the territorial units of the Republic. Frenchmen living outside France shall be represented in the Senate.

ARTICLE 25

An organic law shall determine the term for which each assembly is elected, the number of its members, their emoluments, the conditions of eligibility and ineligibility and the offices incompatible with membership in the assemblies.

It shall likewise determine the conditions under which, in the case of a vacancy in either assembly, persons shall be elected to replace the deputy or senator whose seat has been vacated until the holding of new complete or partial elections to the assembly concerned.

ARTICLE 26

No member of Parliament may be prosecuted, sought, arrested, detained or tried as a result of the opinions or votes expressed by him in the exercise of his functions.

No member of Parliament may, during Parliamentary sessions, be prosecuted or arrested for criminal or minor offenses without the authorization of the assembly of which he is a member except in the case of *flagrante delicto*.

When Parliament is not in session, no member of Parliament may be arrested without the authorization of the Secretariat of the assembly of which he is a member, except in the case of *flagrante delicto*, of authorized prosecution or of final conviction.

The detention or prosecution of a member of Parliament shall be suspended if the assembly of which he is a member so demands.

ARTICLE 27

All binding instructions [upon members of Parliament] shall be null and void.

The right to vote of the members of Parliament shall be personal.

An organic law may, under exceptional circumstances, authorize the delegation of a vote. In this case, no member may be delegated more than one vote.

ARTICLE 28

Parliament shall convene, by right, in two ordinary sessions a year.

The first session shall begin on the first Tuesday of October and shall end on the third Friday of December.

The second session shall open on the last Tuesday of April; it may not last longer than three months.

ARTICLE 29

Parliament shall convene in extraordinary session at the request of the Premier, or of the majority of the members comprising the National Assembly, to consider a specific agenda.

When an extraordinary session is held at the request of the members of the National Assembly, the closure decree shall take effect as soon as the Parliament has exhausted the agenda for which it was called, and at the latest twelve days from the date of its meeting.

Only the Premier may ask for a new session before the end of the month following the closure decree.

ARTICLE 30

Apart from cases in which Parliament meets by right, extraordinary sessions shall be opened and closed by decree of the President of the Republic.

ARTICLE 31

The members of the Government shall have access to the two assemblies. They shall be heard when they so request.

They may call for the assistance of commissioners of the government.

ARTICLE 32

The President of the National Assembly shall be elected for the duration of the legislature. The President of the Senate shall be elected after each partial re-election [of the Senate].

ARTICLE 33

The meetings of the two assemblies shall be public. An *in extenso* report of the debates shall be published in the *Journal Officiel*.

Each assembly may sit in secret committee at the request of the Premier or of one tenth of its members.

Title V

ON RELATIONS BETWEEN PARLIAMENT AND THE GOVERNMENT

ARTICLE 34

All laws shall be passed by Parliament.

Laws shall establish the regulations concerning:

—civil rights and the fundamental guarantees granted to the citizens for the exercise of their public liberties; the obligations imposed by the national defense upon the persons and property of citizens;

—nationality, status and legal capacity of persons, marriage contracts, inheritance and gifts;

—determination of crimes and misdemeanors as well as the penalties imposed therefor, criminal procedure; amnesty; the creation of new juridical systems and the status of magistrates;

—the basis, the rate and the methods of collecting taxes of all types; the issuance of currency.

Laws shall likewise determine the regulations concerning:

—the electoral system of the Parliamentary assemblies and the local assemblies;

—the establishment of categories of public institutions;

—the fundamental guarantees granted to civil and military personnel employed by the State;

—the nationalization of enterprises and the transfer of the property of enterprises from the public to the private sector.

Laws shall determine the fundamental principles of:

—the general organization of national defense;

—the free administration of local communities, the extent of their jurisdiction and their resources;

—education;

—property rights, civil and commercial obligations;

—legislation pertaining to employment, unions and social security.

The financial laws shall determine the financial resources and obligations of the State under the conditions and with the reservations to be provided for by an organic law.

Laws pertaining to national planning shall determine the objectives of the economic and social action of the State.

The provisions of the present article may be developed in detail and amplified by an organic law.

ARTICLE 35

Parliament shall authorize the declaration of war.

ARTICLE 36

Martial law shall be decreed in a meeting of the Council of Ministers.

Its prorogation beyond twelve days may be authorized only by Parliament.

ARTICLE 37

Matters other than those that fall within the domain of law shall be of a regulatory character.

Legislative texts concerning these matters may be modified by decrees issued after consultation with the Council of State. Those legislative texts which may be passed after the present Constitution has become operative shall be modified by decree, only if the Constitutional Council has stated that they have a regulatory character as defined in the preceding paragraph.

ARTICLE 38

The Government may, in order to carry out its program, ask Parliament to authorize it, for a limited period, to take through ordinances measures that are normally within the domain of law.

The ordinances shall be enacted in meetings of the Council of Ministers after consultation with the Council of State. They shall come into force upon their publication, but shall become null and void if the bill for their ratification is not submitted to Parliament before the date set by the enabling act.

At the expiration of the time limit referred to in the first paragraph of the present article, the ordinances may be modified only by law in those matters which are within the legislative domain.

ARTICLE 39

The Premier and the members of Parliament alike shall have the right to initiate legislation.

Government bills shall be discussed in the Council of Ministers after consultation with the Council of State and shall be filed with the Secretariat of one of the two assemblies. Finance bills shall be submitted first to the National Assembly.

ARTICLE 40

Bills and amendments introduced by members of Parliament shall not be considered when their adoption would have as a consequence either a diminution of public financial resources, or the creation or increase of public expenditures.

ARTICLE 41

If it appears in the course of the legislative procedure that a Parliamentary bill or an amendment is not within the domain of law or is contrary to a delegation [of authority] granted by virtue of Article 38, the Government may declare its inadmissibility.

In case of disagreement between the Government and the President of the assembly concerned, the Constitutional Council, upon the request of either party, shall rule within a time limit of eight days.

ARTICLE 42

The discussion of Government bills shall pertain, in the first assembly to which they have been referred, to the text presented by the Government.

An assembly, given a text passed by the other assembly, shall deliberate on the text that is transmitted to it.

ARTICLE 43

Government and Parliamentary bills shall, at the request of the Government or of the assembly concerned, be sent for study to committees especially designated for this purpose.

Government and Parliamentary bills for which such a request has not been made shall be sent to one of the permanent committees, the number of which shall be limited to six in each assembly.

ARTICLE 44

Members of Parliament and of the Government shall have the right of amendment.

After the opening of the debate, the Government may oppose the examination of any amendment which has not previously been submitted to committee.

If the Government so requests, the assembly concerned shall decide, by a single vote, on all or part of the text under discussion, retaining only the amendments proposed or accepted by the Government.

ARTICLE 45

Every Government or Parliamentary bill shall be examined successively in the two assemblies of Parliament with a view to the adoption of an identical text.

When, as a result of disagreement between the two assemblies, it has become impossible to adopt a Government or Parliamentary bill after two readings by each assembly, or, if the Government has declared the matter urgent, after a single reading by each of them, the Premier shall have the right to have a joint committee meet, composed of an equal number from both assemblies and instructed to offer for consideration a text on the matters still under discussion.

The text prepared by the joint committee may be submitted by the Government for approval of the two assemblies. No amendment shall be admissible except by agreement with the Government.

If the joint committee fails to approve a common text, or if this text is not adopted under the conditions set forth in the preceding paragraph, the Government may, after a new reading by the National Assembly and by the Senate, ask the National Assembly to rule definitively. In this case, the National Assembly may reconsider either the text prepared by the joint committee or the last text adopted [by the National Assembly], modified, when circumstances so require, by one or several of the amendments adopted by the Senate.

ARTICLE 46

The laws that the Constitution characterizes as organic shall be passed and amended under the following conditions:

A Government or Parliamentary bill shall be submitted to the deliberation and to the vote of the first assembly to which it is submitted only at the expiration of a period of fifteen days following its introduction.

The procedure of Article 45 shall be applicable. Nevertheless, lacking an agreement between the two assemblies, the text may be adopted by the National Assembly on final reading only by an absolute majority of its members.

The organic laws relative to the Senate must be passed in the same manner by the two assemblies.

Organic laws may be promulgated only after a declaration by the Constitutional Council on their constitutionality.

ARTICLE 47

Parliament shall pass finance bills under the conditions to be stipulated by an organic law.

Should the National Assembly fail to reach a decision on first reading within a time limit of forty days after a bill has been filed, the Government shall refer it to the Senate, which must rule within a time limit of fifteen days. The procedure set forth in Article 45 shall then be followed.

Should Parliament fail to reach a decision within a time limit of seventy days, the provisions of the bill may be enforced by ordinance.

Should the finance bill establishing the resources and expenditures of a fiscal year not be filed in time for it to be promulgated before the beginning of that fiscal year, the Government shall immediately request Parliament for the authorization to collect the taxes and shall make available by decree the funds needed to meet the Government commitments already voted.

The time limits stipulated in the present article shall be suspended when Parliament is not in session.

The Audit Office shall assist Parliament and the Government in supervising the implementation of the finance laws.

ARTICLE 48

The discussion of the bills filed or agreed upon by the Government shall have priority on the agenda of the assemblies in the order set by the Government.

One meeting a week shall be reserved, by priority, for questions asked by members of Parliament and for answers by the Government.

ARTICLE 49

The Premier, after deliberation by the Council of Ministers, may pledge the responsibility of the Government to the National Assembly with regard to the program of the Government, or with regard to a declaration of general policy, as the case may be.

The National Assembly may question the responsibility of the Government by the vote of a motion of censure. Such a motion shall be admissible only if it is signed by at least one tenth of the members of the National Assembly. The vote may only take place forty-eight hours after the motion has been filed; the only votes counted shall be those favorable to the motion of censure, which may be adopted only by a majority of the members comprising the Assembly. Should the motion of censure be rejected, its signatories may not introduce another motion in the course of the same session, except in the case provided for in the paragraph below.

The Premier may, after deliberation by the Council of Ministers, pledge the Government's responsibility to the National Assembly on the vote of a text. In this case, the text shall be considered as adopted, unless a motion of censure, filed in the succeeding twenty-four hours, is voted under the conditions laid down in the previous paragraph.

The Premier shall be entitled to ask the Senate for approval of a general policy declaration.

ARTICLE 50

When the National Assembly adopts a motion of censure, or when it disapproves the program or a declaration of general policy of the Government, the Premier must submit the resignation of the Government to the President of the Republic.

ARTICLE 51

The closure of ordinary or extraordinary sessions shall by right be delayed, should the occasion arise, in order to permit the application of the provisions of Article 49.

Title VI

ON TREATIES AND INTERNATIONAL AGREEMENTS

ARTICLE 52

The President of the Republic shall negotiate and ratify treaties. He shall be informed of all negotiations leading to the conclusion of an international agreement not subject to ratification.

ARTICLE 53

Peace treaties, commercial treaties, treaties or agreements relative to international organization, those that imply a commitment for the finances of the State, those that modify provisions of a legislative nature, those relative to the status of persons, those that call for the cession, exchange or addition of territory may be ratified or approved only by a law.

They shall go into effect only after having been ratified or approved.

No cession, no exchange, no addition of territory shall be valid without the consent of the populations concerned.

ARTICLE 54

If the Constitutional Council, the matter having been referred to it by the President of the Republic, by the Premier, or by the President of one or the other assembly, shall declare that an international commitment contains a clause contrary to the Constitution, the authorization to ratify or approve this commitment may be given only after amendment of the Constitution.

ARTICLE 55

Treaties or agreements duly ratified or approved shall, upon their publication, have an authority superior to that of laws, subject, for each agreement or treaty, to its application by the other party.

Title VII

THE CONSTITUTIONAL COUNCIL

ARTICLE 56

The Constitutional Council shall consist of nine members, whose term of office shall last nine years and shall not be renewable. One third of the membership of the Constitutional Council shall be renewed every three years. Three of its members shall be appointed by the President of the Republic, three by the President of the National Assembly, three by the President of the Senate.

In addition to the nine members provided for above, former Presidents of the Republic shall be members ex officio for life of the Constitutional Council.

The President shall be appointed by the President of the Republic. He shall have the deciding vote in case of a tie.

ARTICLE 57

The office of member of the Constitutional Council shall be incompatible with that of minister or member of Parliament. Other incompatibilities shall be determined by an organic law.

ARTICLE 58

The Constitutional Council shall ensure the regularity of the election of the President of the Republic.

It shall examine complaints and shall announce the results of the vote.

ARTICLE 59

The Constitutional Council shall rule, in the case of disagreement, on the regularity of the election of deputies and senators.

ARTICLE 60

The Constitutional Council shall ensure the regularity of referendum procedures and shall announce the results thereof.

ARTICLE 61

Organic laws, before their promulgation, and regulations of the Parliamentary assemblies, before they come into application, must be submitted to the Constitutional Council, which shall rule on their constitutionality.

To the same end, laws may be submitted to the Constitutional Council, before their promulgation, by the President of the Republic, the Premier or the President of one or the other assembly.

In the cases provided for by the two preceding paragraphs, the Constitutional Council must make its ruling within a time limit of one month. Nevertheless, at the request of the Government, in case of emergency, this period shall be reduced to eight days.

In these same cases, referral to the Constitutional Council shall suspend the time limit for promulgation.

ARTICLE 62

A provision declared unconstitutional may not be promulgated or implemented.

The decisions of the Constitutional Council may not be appealed to any jurisdiction whatsoever. They must be recognized by the governmental authorities and by all administrative and juridical authorities.

ARTICLE 63

An organic law shall determine the rules of organization and functioning of the Constitutional Council, the procedure to be followed before it, and in particular the periods of time allowed for laying disputes before it.

Title VIII

ON
JUDICIAL
AUTHORITY

ARTICLE 64

The President of the Republic shall be the guarantor of the independence of the judicial authority.

He shall be assisted by the High Council of the Judiciary.

An organic law shall determine the status of magistrates.

Magistrates may not be removed from office.

ARTICLE 65

The High Council of the Judiciary shall be presided over by the President of the Republic. The Minister of Justice shall be its Vice President ex officio. He may preside in place of the President of the Republic.

The High Council shall, in addition, include nine members appointed by the President of the Republic in conformity with the conditions to be determined by an organic law.

The High Council of the Judiciary shall present nominations for judges of the Court of Cassation [Supreme Court of Appeal] and for First Presidents of Courts of Appeal. It shall give its opinion, under the conditions to be determined by an organic law, on proposals of the Minister of Justice relative to the nomination of the other judges. It shall be consulted on questions of pardon under conditions to be determined by an organic law.

The High Council of the Judiciary shall act as a disciplinary council for judges. In such cases, it shall be presided over by the First President of the Court of Cassation.

ARTICLE 66

No one may be arbitrarily detained.

The judicial authority, guardian of individual liberty, shall ensure respect for this principle under the conditions stipulated by law.

Title IX

THE HIGH
COURT OF
JUSTICE

ARTICLE 67

A High Court of Justice shall be instituted.

It shall be composed of members [of Parliament] elected, in equal number, by the National Assembly and the Senate after each general or partial election to these assemblies. It shall elect its President from among its members.

An organic law shall determine the composition of the High Court, its rules, and also the procedure to be followed before it.

ARTICLE 68

The President of the Republic shall not be held accountable for actions performed in the exercise of his office except in the case of high treason. He may be indicted only by the two assemblies ruling by identical vote in open balloting and by an absolute majority of the members of said assemblies. He shall be tried by the High Court of Justice.

The members of the Government shall be criminally liable for actions performed in the exercise of their office and deemed to be crimes or misdemeanors at the time they were committed. The procedure defined above shall be applied to them, as well as to their accomplices, in case of a conspiracy against the security of the State. In the cases provided for by the present paragraph, the High Court shall be bound by the definition of crimes and misdemeanors, as well as by the determination of penalties, as they are established by the criminal laws in force when the acts are committed.

Title X

THE
ECONOMIC
AND SOCIAL
COUNCIL

ARTICLE 69

The Economic and Social Council, whenever the Government calls upon it, shall give its opinion on the Government bills, ordinances and decrees, as well as on the Parliamentary bills submitted to it.

A member of the Economic and Social Council may be designated by the latter to present, before the Parliamentary assemblies, the opinion of the Council on the Government or Parliamentary bills that have been submitted to it.

ARTICLE 70

The Economic and Social Council may likewise be consulted by the Government on any problem of an economic or social character of interest to the Republic or to the Community. Any plan, or any bill dealing with a plan, of an economic or social character shall be submitted to it for its advice.

ARTICLE 71

The composition of the Economic and Social Council and its rules of procedure shall be determined by an organic law.

Title XI

ON TERRITORIAL UNITS

ARTICLE 72

The territorial units of the Republic are the communes, the Departments, the Overseas Territories. Other territorial units may be created by law.

These units shall be free to govern themselves through elected councils and under the conditions stipulated by law.

In the departments and the territories, the Delegate of the Government shall be responsible for the national interests, for administrative supervision, and for seeing that the laws are respected.

ARTICLE 73

Measures of adjustment required by the particular situation of the Overseas Departments may be taken with regard to their legislative system and administrative organization.

ARTICLE 74

The Overseas Territories of the Republic shall have a special organization, which takes into account their own interests within the general interests of the Republic. This organization shall be defined and modified by law after consultation with the Territorial Assembly concerned.

ARTICLE 75

Citizens of the Republic who do not have ordinary civil status, the only status referred to in Article 34, may keep their personal status as long as they have not renounced it.

ARTICLE 76

The Overseas Territories may retain their status within the Republic.

If they express the desire to do so by a decision of their Territorial Assemblies taken within the time limit set in the first paragraph of Article 91, they shall become Overseas Departments of the Republic or member States of the Community, either in groups or as single units.

Title XII

ON THE COMMUNITY

ARTICLE 77

In the Community instituted by the present Constitution, the States shall enjoy autonomy; they shall administer themselves and manage their own affairs democratically and freely.

There shall be only one citizenship in the Community.

All citizens shall be equal before the law, whatever their origin, their race and their religion. They shall have the same duties.

ARTICLE 78

The Community's jurisdiction shall extend over foreign policy, defense, currency, common economic and financial policy, as well as over policy on strategic raw materials.

It shall include, in addition, except in the case of specific agreements, the supervision of the tribunals, higher education, the general organization of external transportation and transportation within the Community, as well as of telecommunications.

Special agreements may create other common jurisdictions or regulate any transfer of jurisdiction from the Community to one of its members.

ARTICLE 79

The member States shall benefit from the provisions of Article 77 as soon as they have exercised the choice provided for in Article 76.

Until the measures required for implementation of the present title go into force, matters within the common jurisdiction shall be regulated by the Republic.

ARTICLE 80

The President of the Republic shall preside over and represent the Community.

The institutional organs of the Community shall be an Executive Council, a Senate and a Court of Arbitration.

ARTICLE 81

The member States of the Community shall participate in the election of the President according to the conditions stipulated in Article 6.

The President of the Republic, in his capacity as President of the Community, shall be represented in each State of the Community.

ARTICLE 82

The Executive Council of the Community shall be presided over by the President of the Community. It shall consist of the Premier of the Republic, the heads of Government of each of the member States of the Community, and the ministers responsible for the common affairs of the Community.

The Executive Council shall organize the cooperation of members of the Community at Government and administrative levels.

The organization and procedure of the Executive Council shall be determined by an organic law.

ARTICLE 83

The Senate of the Community shall be composed of delegates whom the Parliament of the Republic and the legislative assemblies of the other members of the Community shall choose from among their own membership. The number of delegates of each State shall be determined according to its population and the responsibilities it assumes in the Community.

The Senate of the Community shall hold two sessions a year, which shall be opened and closed by the President of the Community and may not last longer than one month each.

The Senate of the Community, when called upon by the President of the Community, shall deliberate on the common economic and financial policy before laws on these matters are voted upon by the Parliament of the Republic and, should circumstances so require, by the legislative assemblies of the other members of the Community.

The Senate of the Community shall examine the acts and treaties or international agreements, which are specified in Articles 35 and 53, and which commit the Community.

The Senate of the Community shall make executory decisions in the domains in which it has received delegation of power from the legislative assemblies of the members of the Community. These decisions shall be promulgated in the same form as the law in the territory of each of the States concerned.

An organic law shall determine the composition of the Senate and its rules of procedure.

ARTICLE 84

A Court of Arbitration of the Community shall rule on litigations occurring among members of the Community.

Its composition and its jurisdiction shall be determined by an organic law.

ARTICLE 85

Be derogation from the procedure provided for in Article 89, the provisions of the present title that concern the functioning of the common institutions shall be amendable by identical laws passed by the Parliament of the Republic and by the Senate of the Community.

ARTICLE 86

A change of status of a member State of the Community may be requested, either by the Republic, or by a resolution of the legislative assembly of the State concerned confirmed by a local referendum, the organization and supervision of which shall be ensured by the institutions of the Community. The procedures governing this change shall be determined by an agreement approved by the Parliament of the Republic and the legislative assembly concerned.

Under the same conditions, a member State of the Community

may become independent. It shall thereby cease to belong to the Community.

ARTICLE 87

The special agreements made for the implementation of the present title shall be approved by the Parliament of the Republic and the legislative assembly concerned.

Title XIII

ON AGREEMENTS OF ASSOCIATION

ARTICLE 88

The Republic or the Community may make agreements with States that wish to associate themselves with the Community in order to develop their own civilizations.

Title XIV

ON AMENDMENT

ARTICLE 89

The initiative for amending the Constitution shall belong both to the President of the Republic on the proposal of the Premier and to the members of Parliament.

The Government or Parliamentary bill for amendment must be passed by the two assemblies in identical terms. The amendment shall become definitive after approval by a referendum.

Nevertheless, the proposed amendment shall not be submitted to a referendum when the President of the Republic decides to submit it to Parliament convened in Congress; in this case, the proposed amendment shall be approved only if it is accepted by a three-fifths majority of the votes cast. The Secretariat of the Congress shall be that of the National Assembly.

No amendment procedure may be undertaken or followed when the integrity of the territory is in jeopardy.

The republican form of government shall not be subject to amendment.

Title XV

TEMPORARY
PROVISIONS

ARTICLE 90

The ordinary session of Parliament is suspended. The mandate of the members of the present National Assembly shall expire on the day that the Assembly elected under the present Constitution convenes.

Until this meeting, the Government alone shall have the authority to convene Parliament.

The mandate of the members of the Assembly of the French Union shall expire at the same time as the mandate of the members of the present National Assembly.

ARTICLE 91

The institutions of the Republic, provided for by the present Constitution, shall be established within four months after its promulgation.

This time limit shall be extended to six months for the institutions of the Community.

The powers of the President of the Republic now in office shall expire only when the results of the election provided for in Articles 6 and 7 of the present Constitution are proclaimed.

The member States of the Community shall participate in this first election under the conditions derived from their status at the date of the promulgation of the Constitution.

The established authorities shall continue to exercise their functions in these States according to the laws and regulations applicable when the Constitution becomes operative, until the authorities provided for by their new regimes are set up.

Until it is definitively constituted, the Senate shall consist of the present members of the Council of the Republic. The organic laws that determine the definitive composition of the Senate must be passed before July 31, 1959.

The powers conferred on the Constitutional Council by Articles 58 and 59 of the Constitution shall be exercised, until this Council is set up, by a committee composed of the Vice President of the Council of State, as chairman, the First President of the Court of Cassation, and the First President of the Audit Office.

The peoples of the member States of the Community shall continue to be represented in Parliament until the measures necessary to the implementation of Title XII have been put into effect.

ARTICLE 92

The legislative measures necessary for the setting up of the institutions and, until they are set up, for the functioning of the governmental authorities, shall be taken in meetings of the Council of Ministers, after consultation with the Council of State, in the form of ordinances having the force of law.

During the time limit set in the first paragraph of Article 91, the Government shall be authorized to determine, by ordinances having the force of law and passed in the same way, the system of elections to the assemblies provided for by the Constitution.

During the same period and under the same conditions, the Government may also adopt measures, in all matters, which it may deem necessary to the life of the nation, the protection of citizens or the safeguarding of liberties.

INDEX